PRACTICE THESE PRINCIPLES

⁓ and ⁓

WHAT IS THE OXFORD GROUP?

PRACTICE THESE
PRINCIPLES

∽ *and* ∽

WHAT IS
THE OXFORD
GROUP?

With a Foreword by

SUE SMITH WINDOWS,
daughter of Dr. Bob Smith,
cofounder of Alcoholics Anonymous

HAZELDEN
HP
PITTMAN
Archives
Press

■ HAZELDEN®

INFORMATION & EDUCATIONAL SERVICES

Hazelden
Center City, Minnesota 55012-0176
1-800-328-9000 (Toll Free U.S., Canada, and the Virgin Islands)
1-651-213-4000 (Outside the U.S. and Canada)
1-651-213-4590 (24-hour Fax)
http://www.hazelden.org (World Wide Web site on Internet)

ISBN: 1-56838-150-6

01 00   6 5 4

Book design by Connie G. Baker
Cover design by David Spohn

In gratitude to Jo Ann Browning
and Don Browning, M.D.,
of Little Rock, Arkansas,
who donated the funds for the
production of this book.

CONTENTS

*A*s I grew up during my teen years, my mother, Anne Smith, held steadfast to the hope and dream that her husband, Dr. Bob Smith, would become a sober, changed individual, which certainly did happen eventually. But it was a long, hard journey. In the early 1930s, Mother saw a faint glimmer of hope at last, due in large part to the love and fellowship she received from the Oxford Group in Akron, Ohio.

Because the Oxford Group and the book *What Is the Oxford Group?* dramatically and positively changed the course of my family's life, not to mention the millions of other lives that have been and continue to be changed by Alcoholics Anonymous, I will always feel immense love and gratitude toward this wonderful organization of supportive individuals.

I am, therefore, honored that I have been asked to write the foreword to this book, which consists of a reprinting of the original *What Is the Oxford Group?* and a modern-day revision, titled *Practice These Principles.*

That "faint glimmer of hope" I mentioned earlier proved to be a nibble of things to come for my mother. I could put it another way and say that Anne Smith snatched at what the Oxford Group had to offer much like a largemouth bass takes to a night crawler. She was solely intent on clinging to and strengthening the one facet that gave her life its true meaning: HOPE.

Mother faithfully attended Oxford Group meetings and read copiously about the subject areas and authors of special interest to members. Through sharing and receiving the sharing of others, she learned how to cope and live more serenely than she ever thought possible. By no means was any of this an easy course to follow, but it was very satisfying in the long run, as many AA members would certainly testify.

Another huge source of support my mother received was through the many long phone calls she had with Oxford Group members, most notably Henrietta Seiberling, who was instrumental in arranging the first meeting between Bill Wilson and my father.

My mother and fellow Oxford Group members worked together to get Dad to attend meetings and eventually to share his alcohol problem with the group. Dad came to rely on the love, support, and praise he received from the Oxford Group. And, after he met Bill W., he went into full gear with the Four Absolutes.

In those days, when a person had a slip — such as when Bill W. slipped after Ebby Thacher talked with him, and when Dad slipped after meeting with Bill W. — there were no guidelines to follow in order to rectify the slip, except for the Four Absolutes. Bill W. and Dr. Bob pounded out the Twelve Steps of Alcoholics Anonymous after they had attended Oxford Group meetings over the course of three years. As a result, the principles embodied in the Twelve Steps come primarily through Bill's and Dad's involvement in the Oxford Group.

My father , who died in 1950, took his last drink June 10, 1935. The years of sobriety he enjoyed were due to the influence of the Oxford Group and, later, Alcoholics Anonymous. Both of these groups allowed my mother's hope and dream to come true.

It is my hope and dream that many, many people who have diverse problems and are in need of solace and support, as well as those who have a keen interest in expanding their recovery programs, will benefit from these two books within a book (which in essence is a *primer* of the Oxford Group), just as my parents and early AA members have benefited from it.

All of us can apply the principles contained in *Practice These Principles* and *What Is the Oxford Group?* to our daily lives and, as a result, form a closer relationship to our idea of God.

—SUE SMITH WINDOWS
AKRON, OHIO

INTRODUCTION

A.A.'s Twelve Steps are a group of principles,
spiritual in their nature,
which, if practiced as a way of life,
can expel the obsession to drink
and enable the sufferer to become happy and usefully whole.
—TWELVE STEPS AND TWELVE TRADITIONS

I spoke at an AA group's anniversary meeting in St. Paul, Minnesota, about a year ago and left the members with a riddle, "If the principles of Twelve Step recovery are not the Twelve Steps, then what are the principles?"

I returned to the same meeting recently to present a sponsee with a sobriety medallion and a few people approached me with the same comment. "I've been looking all year, since your talk, in the literature for the principles and can't find them!" My answer was the same as I tell my sponsees, "The *principles* of Twelve Step recovery are the opposite of our character defects."

In recovery, we try to take the opposite of our character defects/shortcomings and turn them into principles. For example, we work to change fear into faith, hate into love, egoism into humility, anxiety and worry into serenity, complacency into action, denial into acceptance, jealousy into trust, fantasizing into reality, selfishness into service, resentment into forgiveness, judgmentalism into tolerance, despair into hope, self-hate into self-respect, and loneliness into fellowship. Through this work we learn to understand the principles of our program.

Such work may look like an overwhelming goal to an outsider, but those of us in AA know that our true goal is "progress, not perfection." As the Big Book, *Alcoholics Anonymous*, tells us, we are not destined for sainthood and we should not be discouraged when we cannot "maintain anything like perfect adherence to these principles. The point is, that we are willing to grow along spiritual lines. The principles are guides to progress."

But what, exactly, are these principles and where did they come from? Over the years a list of principles that correspond to each of the Twelve Steps has been printed in local area AA newsletters and on pocket cards. The origin of this list is unknown, although used by many Twelve Step members:

STEP 1	HONESTY
STEP 2	HOPE
STEP 3	FAITH
STEP 4	COURAGE
STEP 5	INTEGRITY
STEP 6	WILLINGNESS
STEP 7	HUMILITY
STEP 8	BROTHERLY LOVE
STEP 9	JUSTICE
STEP 10	PERSEVERANCE
STEP 11	SPIRITUAL AWARENESS
STEP 12	SERVICE

The origins of AA's principles, and of the AA program itself, can be traced back to the Oxford Group, a nondenominational spiritual movement. The cofounders of AA, Bill Wilson and Dr. Bob Smith, were both associated with the Oxford Group prior to their meeting in 1935. (Bill attended meetings for five months and Dr. Bob for two and a half years.) The Oxford Group's influence on the development of AA was substantial. As Bill Wilson wrote in *Alcoholics Anonymous Comes of Age*, "The important thing is this: the early A.A. got its ideas of self-examination, acknowledgment of character defects, restitution for harm done, and working with others straight from the Oxford Groups." Today millions of individuals and their families have been helped by AA's suggested Twelve Step program, which originated primarily from the Oxford Group. Also, other Twelve Step fellowships (e.g., Narcotics Anonymous, Al-Anon, Overeaters Anonymous) have helped countless others improve their lives.

What Is the Oxford Group?, written anonymously in 1933, is considered to be the "Big Book" of the Oxford Group and its reprinting here is offered for those interested in the historic roots of the Twelve Steps, principles of AA, and as a study guide. *What Is the Oxford Group?* appears here in its entire original version, although the page numbers in this reprint do not correspond to the original. *Practice These Principles* is a revision of the original 1933 book with more up-to-date secular language. Studying these books can only add a greater perspective of the principles of Twelve Step recovery.

That the Oxford Group influenced the structure of Alcoholics Anonymous is common knowledge within the program. What has not always been told or recognized are the details of the spiritual recovery material that Bill W. and Dr. Bob heard, learned, and applied from the Oxford Group. Many of the ideas that formed the foundation of AA's suggested Steps of recovery came from (the then named) A First Century Christian Fellowship—founded in 1921 by a Lutheran minister, Dr. Frank Buchman, and led in New York by his chief American lieutenant, Rev. Samuel Shoemaker, rector of

Calvary Episcopal Church. This fellowship changed its name to the Oxford Group in 1928.

I suggested earlier that the principles of AA are the opposite of our character defects and one can write quite a list. But basically the principles come directly from the Oxford Group's "Four Absolutes" (absolute honesty, absolute purity, absolute unselfishness, and absolute love).

It would have been very awkward for the AA program to include the Four Absolutes in their Big Book and would have not, in a sense, indicated a marked split from the Oxford Group. This is not to say that the founders of AA did not respect and value the role the Four Absolutes had in the development of AA's suggested program of recovery. In 1948, Dr. Bob recalled the absolutes as "the only yardsticks" Alcoholics Anonymous had in the early days, before the Twelve Steps. He said he still felt they could be extremely helpful when he wanted to do the right thing and the answer was not obvious. "Almost always, if I measure my decision carefully by the yardsticks of absolute honesty, absolute unselfishness, absolute purity, and absolute love, and it checks up pretty well with those four, then my answer can't be very far out of the way," he said. The absolutes form the basis for many AA meetings around America today and are still published and widely quoted in the Ohio area.

Many men and women found recovery from alcoholism in the Oxford Group. Another AA forefather who originally found guidance in the Oxford Group was Richmond Walker. He stayed sober with the help of the Oxford Group in Boston, Massachusetts. Richmond, who later came to AA, would write the most famous and often used daily meditation book for Twelve Step recovery, *Twenty-Four Hours a Day*.

During the writing of AA's Big Book, Bill W. and other contributors developed a more specific "Oxfordized" method of helping only alcoholics. They deleted aspects of Oxford Group ideas which, in their experience, did not apply, such as showing a lack of anonymity, requiring a newcomer to accept his alcoholism, referring to God by a specific name (Jesus), and placing emphasis on attracting famous people to the fellowship. Also, early AA members added Dr. William Silkworth's ideas about alcoholism that are detailed in the Big Book chapters "The Doctor's Opinion" and "More About Alcoholism." These ideas account for Step One of the Twelve Steps of Alcoholics Anonymous. Some of the ideas about spiritual experience and spiritual awakening came from the American psychologist William James, outlined in his book *The Varieties of Religious Experience*, published in 1902, and used extensively by Oxford Group members.

In a March 1960 article titled "After Twenty-Five Years," which appeared *The A.A. Grapevine*, Bill W. wrote:

> *William James also heavily emphasized the need for hitting bottom. Thus did he reinforce A.A.'s Step One and so did he supply us with the spiritual essence of today's Step Twelve. Having now accounted for A.A.'s Step One and Twelve, it is natural that we should ask, "Where did the early A.A.s find the material for the remaining ten Steps? Where did we learn about moral inventory, amends for harm done, turning wills and lives over to God? Where did we learn about meditation and prayer and all the rest of it?" The spiritual substance of our remaining ten Steps came straight from Dr. Bob's and my own earlier association with the Oxford Groups.*

During the same period that Bill W. was writing AA's Big Book, the early AAs were slowly ending their association with the Oxford Group, first in New York and gradually in Akron. The primary reasons that the (yet unnamed) AA's left the Oxford Group were (1) they wanted to concentrate on only helping alcoholics, (2) the Oxford Group leader, Frank Buchman, made favorable comments in public about Nazi Germany, (3) the Catholic Church discouraged its members from joining any other "religious" groups, which the Oxford Group was perceived to be, and (4) the Oxford Group frowned on tobacco use.

One often hears that early AA's left the Oxford Group due to the group's dislike and unwillingness to help alcoholics. The following excerpt from Charles Clapp's book *The Big Bender* illustrates the opposite. Clapp writes of an incident that occurred four months after Bill W. and Dr. Bob met:

> *It was not long before I was again on a bender of three days' duration. The third loop occurred in early October and I landed in town (New York City) before it had ended. There, a former drunk who had completely given up drinking after coming in touch with the Oxford Group, cornered me. We spent several hours together and I honestly faced not only the problem of liquor itself, but all the things underneath and back of it all, which had caused me to drink. For the first time, I admitted drinking had me licked; when I drank I lost control of myself and I was the most selfish human being on earth. I definitely determined to turn my life over to God, to try and straighten out all the messes I had caused and to pay whatever price was necessary to get my life, as nearly as I could, on a basis of Absolute Honesty, Purity, Unselfishness, and Love. Since that day in October, 1935, I have not had a drink. . . .*

One way to test quickly a thought or plan is to see if it conflicts with any one of the four standards—Absolute Honesty, Absolute Purity, Absolute Unselfishness, and Absolute Love. It is a certainty God is not going to tell me to do anything which will violate any of these. Should a thought or plan of great moment, or one about which there was some doubt come to me, I check it with others who are living on this basis. Checking is done by talking it all over, clearly and honestly, praying about it, and seeing whether it seems right. . . .

I have not become absolutely honest, pure, unselfish, and loving—no, nowhere near! But whereas I used to be a drunk—now I don't drink at all; I used to think of no one but myself—now I endeavor to be considerate of others; I used to lie when I felt like it—now I try to tell the truth; I used to look down on most people—now I see qualities in them which I never knew existed; I used to be restless and unhappy—now I am calm and happy; I used to think the other fellow was always wrong— now I do not; I used to feel that conditions, times, the town, the state, the country, and the world were at fault and should be changed—now I realize it is individuals like myself who need to change.

In this way of life I am very new. The sample I have tasted is swell—I want more. In seeking and following this new path I do not know where I may go, what I may do, how I may live, or what I may become, but I do know that I have found a formula for my own life which works better than any I have known. Believe me, from where I sit, the future looks fascinating—full of adventure, action, romance, happiness, and tremendous hope.

I was fortunate to complete a one thousand-hour internship for my master's degree in the archives at AA headquarters in New York City in 1983. This was an invaluable experience as my subsequent career has remained in archival and historical research and writing about what America has done regarding alcoholism and its treatment during the past two hundred years. Also, as an AA member, I felt honored to meet many of the individuals who participated in and remembered the period between 1935 and 1939. My personal recovery has been enriched by the research I've done of the Oxford Group and its influence in the putting together of AA's Big Book.

In my own bias and as a student of the Big Book, I believe we all may benefit by studying the history of AA. This presentation of *What Is the Oxford Group?* and *Practice These Principles* will help readers understand the significant role the Oxford Group had in the development of Alcoholics Anonymous.

I suggest that fellow members and sponsees who read this 1933 Big Book of the Oxford Group take notes while reading and write down similarities between *What Is the Oxford Group?* and the Big Book of Alcoholics Anonymous (third edition). Examples:

1.   "Half measures availed us nothing."
     Alcoholics Anonymous, p. 59

     "Half measures will be as fruitless as
     no measures at all."
     What Is the Oxford Group?, pp. 33–34

2.   "The age of miracles is still with us."
     Alcoholics Anonymous, p. 153

     "The age of miracles is still with us."
     What Is the Oxford Group?, p. 61

3.   "So our troubles, we think, are basically
     of our own making."
     Alcoholics Anonymous, p. 62

     "Difficulties in the way are your own making."
     What Is the Oxford Group?, p. 113

The three examples cited above are only a beginning of the study opportunities in this exercise. Be sure to look at the chapter on "Guidance" in *What Is the Oxford Group?* (pages 57–63) and pages 68, 86–87, and 95 in AA's Big Book. In addition to the Four Absolutes, the Oxford Group practiced the principles of the "Five C's": confidence, confession, conviction, conversion, and continuance. One can find an explanation of the Five C's in another book written by an Oxford Group turned AA member, Richmond Walker, in his book *Twenty-Four Hours a Day* (May 23rd through May 27th).

I would like to thank my friends in Little Rock, Arkansas, for their assistance and suggestions while I worked on the *Practice These Principles* text.

—BILL P.

PRACTICE

THESE

PRINCIPLES

Book I

CONTENTS

OUR FELLOWSHIP

Our Fellowship has no official membership list, subscriptions, badge, or rules, nor owns vast amounts of property. It is a name for a group of people who, from every rank, profession, and trade, in many countries, have surrendered their lives to the God of their understanding. They are endeavoring to lead spiritual lives under the guidance of the Spirit of the Universe.

Our Fellowship is not a religion. It has no hierarchy, no temples, no endowments; its members have no salaries, no plans but God's plan. Every country is their country, every person their brother and sister. They carry our message in modern dress, wearing spiritual armor. Their aim is to realize their suggested program of recovery on the world tide of addiction.

Our Fellowship works within every religious denomination, planning to bring those outside back into their fold and to reawaken those within to their *maximum* service to God. It advocates nothing that is not the fundamental basis of all religious faiths and takes no side in sectarian disputes. It seeks to enable us to use our beliefs to their best advantage for ourselves and for the world in general. This means living as near as we can, by God's help, to the lives our Higher Power has mapped out for us. When we decide to accept this new way of living we can get back to that plan again by surrendering our lives to the God of our understanding. By our good works we live as parallel as we can to Right Principles here on earth. With God's Guidance to show us how we can best do that, we can continue on that plan and make progress.

Those of us who have seen the wonders of the results of the life changing of new members can only describe them as modern miracles. These are men and women who have never before realized that self-will can kill not only the soul but also mind, talents, and happiness as surely as a malignant cancer can kill the body. They have found that surrender to God, in actuality as well as in theory, means a new lease on life that brings with it a fuller joy of living than they ever realized was possible. They have been reborn to the world as well as reborn to a Spirit of the Universe.

All their appreciation of the best and worthwhile things in life, of their work, and of their capacity for human friendship have become really alive. Living has now limitless depth and breadth and height and is no longer a stifling prison. A Higher Power has ceased to be only a figure in religion to them and becomes a Reality with boundless modern wisdom, an understanding and really helpful Creative Intelligence who is very near to them in all they think, do, and say. They know now the secret of real happiness on earth, the spiritual profit given by the right kind of outlook, a real sense of the values of life, and a true sense of spiritual and material proportion. In fact, they have become sane.

Undeniable evidence of the fruits of the work of our Fellowship has been published and needs no repetition here. Books detailing many of the marvels that have resulted from its changing of lives can be obtained easily. Spoken evidence from men and women witnesses can be heard at weekly meetings or at larger gatherings, which are arranged from time to time in various places. Thousands of these witnesses are convicted by the evidence in their own lives of what the life changing of the program has done for them and can do for others. We will go anywhere at any time to help anyone whose life has become a burden of addiction. We will stand by until that person has been set free from trouble and brought to a new understanding of the spiritual and the possibilities of a new way of life. No person has sunk too far; no case for spiritual care can go beyond our scope. People's knowledge of their need and having a need for change in their lives is all that is necessary for us to help them. We know for sure that the age of miracles has not passed from us. For these miracles we are willing instruments for a willing God.

Families, relationships, and marriages have been united, partners brought together with a new, understanding love between them. Lonely people have been made to see that many are eager for and will be honored by their friendship. People who are obsessed by their problems find that they can be set free and reborn into spiritual liberty. Would-be suicides live to be useful and happy men and women. The young find a purpose in their future, which is not dull and uninteresting but adventurous and worth growing toward. The elderly learn that each day more of life given to them is a day they can live to its fullest. We learn that all vain regrets for our past are as useless as a storm that has passed over and is gone.

The suggested ideals of our Fellowship are to bring into the world the realization of the power of our principles as a force for spiritual and material stability and betterment of the world and to awaken in us as individuals the knowledge that we are wasting our spiritual inheritance and that our active addiction and self-will run riot are the frustration of God's plan for us. It sets out to make the world understand that spiritual common sense is of more practical value and use to humanity than selfish piety or blind paganism.

The working beliefs of the Group are not misty ideals. They are practical standards within the scope of anyone who will give his or her life in the world—powerful, insignificant, interesting, or prosaic as that life may be—into God's absolute keeping. There is no reason why this giving of our lives to God should mean our being pious or religious bores. Neither should it mean that we have to give up our ordinary obligations or duties. It means we surrender to our Higher Power everything that stands between God and us.

Our Fellowship has four points that, we suggest, are the keys to the kind of spiritual life God wishes us to lead. These points are

1. Absolute Honesty

2. Absolute Purity

3. Absolute Unselfishness

4. Absolute Love

The average newcomer on seeing these points or hearing of them asks: "But how can I—or anyone—be absolutely honest or pure or unselfish or loving in a world like this?"

The great spiritual teachers throughout world history have kept to these four points in their fullness. Many were individuals without home, possessions, or earthly commitments. The nearer we live and the progress we make to the Absolute in these four points, the nearer we are to the realm of the Spirit, whether it means being without a home, possessions, or earthly responsibilities, or taking on more responsibilities. God knows the energy we put into our fight for a life founded on Right Principles. God knows the difficulties of circumstances and the influence of environment that confront us at every step. Because God can gauge the sincerity of our vision, our new employer does not too harshly condemn our stumbling. We have not the knowledge that would enable us to judge if any man or woman has been able to live a life absolutely as the saints would have him or her live it. But we do know that these necessary four points for a spiritual life are absolute ones and examples to which we can aspire and make progress, by the help of God.

The four points are the basis of beauty of thought, word, and deed. They may not be so unattainable as we may suppose, although few can or have ever lived lives of Absolute Honesty, Purity, Unselfishness, and Love. "For all have sinned and come short of the glory of God," the Christian writer Saint Paul tells us. It is doubtful if even a mystic, giving up his or her life to pious contemplation, lives a life founded on these four points in their fullness. It is a matter of argument whether their shutting themselves away from human contact is Absolute Love for their fellows. It certainly seems to the uninitiated to be selflessness in a negative form.

The saints and spiritual leaders of this world, past and present, are those who, while still leading a helpful material life for other people, fight relentless warfare against their own temptations and the negative results of character defects in other people. They are the Saint Georges, who persistently strive to kill the dragon of Sin, which will not lie down and die gracefully. Daily they are singed by the fiery breath from the dragon's devouring jaws, crushed to earth by its huge unwieldy body. But they rise again, pick up the sword of a new life dropped when they fell into trouble, and forgiven their fall, by God's grace they commence once again their fight for Honesty, Purity, Unselfishness, and Love.

To be spiritually reborn and to live in the state in which these four points are the suggested guides to our lives in God, we advocate four practical spiritual activities:

1. Sharing our moral inventory and temptations with God and with another person whose life has been given to God, and carrying the message to help others, still unchanged, to recognize and acknowledge their wrongs.

2. Surrender of our lives, past, present, and future, into God's keeping and direction.

3. Restitution to all whom we have wronged directly or indirectly.

4. Listening to, accepting, relying on God's and our
    sponsors', spiritual advisors', fellow members'
    Guidance and carrying it out in everything we do
    or say, great or small.

These spiritual activities have proved indispensable to
countless numbers who are living Changed lives. They are not
new ideas or inventions of our Fellowship. They are the simple
tenets of simple universal spiritual wisdom through time.

Our Fellowship is not one group. It is a collection of groups
active in carrying the message in many countries, meeting in
ordinary places where ordinary men and women are accustomed to meet in the course of their daily lives. We do not
find it necessary to hide. Our mission is the redemption of
individuals and nations from the pain of addiction and to
keep alive the Great Fact that every man, woman, and child in
this world might see and understand that Perfection of Life to
which all of us would attain if we, too, would be spiritually fit.

Our meetings are held everywhere, in small towns and big
cities. When our members share their experiences of a new
way of living, it awakens others to the possibilities of what this
new quality of life may have in store for them. By the help of
God and our fellow members, plans are formed to bring those
who are spiritually asleep or in spiritual need into the Program,
and the best ways to carry these out are discussed.

Action for Good Works is joy to our groups. The utter
belief and full realization of an individual's present pressing
need to change is our incentive. The Groups may be large or
small. But however small they may be, they are vital beacons
of the Sunlight of The Spirit in a fast darkening world.

To those who are strangers to our Program of action, a
meeting is the simplest and most informative means for seeing
the effects and getting to the best understanding of our work.
Also, conventions and assemblies are held at certain intervals
in various states and countries. These large gatherings are not
in the nature of religious conventions, nor are they revivalist

meetings. Newcomers are treated with respect. They meet on an equal social footing, whatever may be their social status elsewhere. Gloom is conspicuous by its absence, and there is more laughter at these gatherings than at many ordinary social gatherings.

At meetings, the God of our understanding is discussed with such a freedom from empty piety that the newcomer, unaware perhaps of the methods of our Fellowship, is often staggered and perplexed before becoming enthralled by the desire to probe deeper into the healthy aspect of the Spirituality of our Program. Individual spiritual needs are attended to in a sensible and businesslike way. The concerns, problems, and happiness of our lives are discussed directly and constructively, without partisanship. All are allowed to contribute their views, for before all is the possibility that God will grant many of those present the opportunity to help others in or out of the Program.

Literature is studied at meetings for its bearing on our individual and collective needs. Mixed meetings are held for sharing our stories and discussion. There are special meetings where women are in close counsel with women, men with men, clergy with clergy, members of a particular profession with other members of that profession, people of one locality with others of the same, inhabitants of a country with their compatriots. Attendance at any organized religious service that may be arranged at a local place of worship is not compulsory for members. Members of a faith attend the services of that faith as that faith demands or as their religious convictions dictate.

The social aspect of our meetings are not forgotten. All are free to do as they wish, to come as they please and go when they want. To the stranger, a meeting—cosmopolitan in nature and with social equality and perfect fellowship—is a glimpse of what the foundation might be of a new, spiritually centered life.

Our members do not set themselves up to be a collection

of paragons of the Virtues, nor are they a set of religious bores. They are the normal men and women we would meet on different occasions and who would no more ram religion down our throats than we would ram it down theirs. They might suggest, as calmly as they might ask us to pass the salt, that God had guided them to speak to us because, by that means, they have become aware that we are in spiritual trouble and need help. If, in reply, we looked at them as if we suspected they were mad, it would neither shake their poise nor damp their cheerful attempt to carry the message. Because they themselves are not saints, they have made the world's *love and service* a common bond for humanity.

Pressure, religious hysteria, and shaming are banned entirely by the Program. We have no use for them. The business of the Fellowship is to eradicate negative behavior from people and so set life free for Absolute Honesty of living. We know by experience that Absolute Love can conquer all evil; that Absolute Truth is as personally necessary for those who speak it as it is for those it is spoken to; that too much dependency on other people for our happiness is weakness; and that fellowship with our fellow members and God is strength.

The Fellowship may be reviled and persecuted. Material antispiritualists and intellectual hypocrites will mock it. But because it is founded on the intrinsic universal simple spiritual truths and is walking bravely toward the Light, it will survive and grow stronger.

SURRENDER

Surrender to God is our actual passing from our old lives of negative behavior to lives that are God-Guided and God-Conscious. In other words, it is the giving up of our old ideas and taking on lives of spiritual activity in everything we think, do, or say. It is making complete restitution for wrongs done to others as we may presently know. We only know that willpower ensures that all debts are paid. By ending all wrong associations, a Changed life renounces entirely all the faults of its spiritual past.

Surrender is our abandonment of our old selves and an endeavoring to live by God's Guidance. Life changing is not idealistic claptrap—as some doubters would term it—but a true change, the wonder of the results of which are provable beyond doubt.

Surrendering our lives to God means a complete giving back to God the negative willpower we have been using, which has separated us by our shortcomings from the Giver. It means taking in its place our Higher Power's will as our will if we would choose to practice these principles.

Willpower is acknowledged to be an active force, as positive in its effects as electricity, for example. These effects and their extensions are beyond present knowledge. We only know that willpower has been the driving force for actual accomplishments of great works, deeds, feats, and inventions, and that if the positive willpower behind them is sufficient, seemingly impossible things can be carried to completion. The willpower for the accomplishment of great achievements in the past has come from God. The willpower of our Fellowship, if it be put under God's Direction, has boundless possibilities. Surrendering our will to God does not mean that our faculties are thereby deadened. Instead they are awakened with the infinite power of God behind them and with the direction of our Higher Power's judgment for their best use—according to the individual plan God has mapped out for each of us.

Our decision to turn our will over to the God of our understanding should be so complete that the phrase "In God we live, we move, and have our being" will be actual. This is not a dream we should like to think possible if we had the spiritual strength or the visionary power of some of the world's famous spiritual leaders. If we honestly surrender our lives to God and immediately begin to rely with love on God's will for the future progress of our surrendered lives, this is a possible state for all of us. This is such a simple fact that it appears complicated to many—as simple facts sometimes do. But, in spite of sounding simple, Surrender is one of the few things in our lives that cannot be done for us. No one can stand in for us. It is an act that can be performed only by the individual. No universal rite, qualifying condition, or set ceremony exists that can take its place. It is our own personal and individual Surrender to God, sudden and more often gradual. Long "foxhole" prayers, excuses for our past, or ego-based expectations wished for the future are not of the least use. To God who knows each one of us far better than we could ever know ourselves, the spirit is of far more importance than the letter. We either *do* or *do not* make the decision to surrender our will and lives. As far as this step is concerned, that is all there is to it.

The word *converted* is confusing to some people. It savors of religious hysteria, old-fashioned revivalism, the latest religious fervor, or dramatic penitent-form scenes—which serve a useful purpose for those whom only such scenes can awaken to a living God. But the word *conversion* itself, although not in frequent use by our Fellowship, is a good one. There is no reason why any of us who want to use it should refrain from doing so if it is our idea of Surrender. But some may choose "spiritual awakening" instead of Surrender to God. We have found that conversion is a definite constructive spiritual principle that ensures it being of positive use and growth for us and for others.

Conversion, Surrender, or if we choose to name it our Spiritual Awakening, is a realization that our lives are out of harmony with our Spiritual selves. It is a determination to live better spiritual lives and our faith that God can and will take from us all our character defects and make our future as if our past had never been. But in addition, Surrender needs our sure and certain conviction that when we are "converted" and God takes control of our lives, our Higher Power will Guide them and we shall increasingly feel that refreshing state of living that shall come with the presence of the Great Reality within us.

Quite a number of us quarrel over the use of a certain word to describe a situation or an act. To some, *Surrender* is the wrong word to use for the Changing—or the "conversion," or our spiritual awakening—of our lives from ego direction to God's Direction. At first many of us visualize our decision as a showing of the white flag, the confessing of defeat to an enemy more powerful than ourselves, and the asking for a truce, perhaps at any cost. To those of us who think like that, Surrender is definitely a weak and cowardly action. We say we would rather go on to the end, like tried and proven trusty soldiers, and then pay the cost, if any, that is due from us. Capitulation never was and never will be in our fighting code. We have, we say, never laid down our arms to an enemy, and never will. But, if any of you want to get support for your weaknesses because you are not ready to live your own life, go ahead and get it if it gives you any pleasure or satisfaction. Only leave us out of your Surrender-to-God business, please!

How fine we feel, those of us who talk and think like that!

We really think of God as a far away, fault-finding Deity whose demands, if we gave in to them or took too much notice of them, would make life, which is already difficult enough, almost unbearable. Although we may not always put it in so many words, it is strange how many of us think on these lines. It is not surprising, therefore, that those who have this conception of a Higher Power take submission to God to signify a cowardly act, when all the time it is a courageous decision to do a courageous thing.

It takes little or no courage to be self-centered, proud of independence and self-will. It needs a tremendous amount of courage to make the decision in which are the very roots of our being and to live a new way of life to the best of our spiritual ability. The courage of those who resign their lives to God is not the land of courage understood by those who find fault with the word *Surrender*. It is spiritual courage, possible to every man and every woman, which means the sacrifice of our confidence and our pride in the material ego. Only those who have surrendered know that it does not mean cringing or apologizing but with courageous optimism, joining God and our brothers and sisters in this spiritual Fellowship.

Our initial Surrender to God does not mean that henceforth we shall be asleep to the world around us. It does not mean that temptations will never challenge or character defects conquer us again, or that, if they do, God is not living up to God's part of the compact. It does not mean that, because we are not willing enough always to be making progress, it is hopeless to think that we cannot continue to live under God's Direction. It means that after Surrender, we have to work and eat and sleep and laugh and play as before, and that in the round of daily life come situations that cause reactions against our spiritual good resolutions. It would be foolish for any of us to pretend that human nature is otherwise. Shortcomings remain short-comings. But even if we surrendered to God only yesterday, our shortcomings of today do not cancel that initial and continuous surrender. God knows and waits.

God waits to see if we will Surrender today's mistakes and shortcomings to our Higher Power with as much sincerity as we took personal inventory of our lives yesterday. God waits to see if we will acknowledge it was lack of trust that made us fail to ask God to take that character defect away from us while it was still temptation, to see if we will take inventory that it was lack of our conscious contact that made us vulnerable to spiritual weakness.

Many newcomers lose heart quickly and say they are not strong enough to carry out what they may call their "Good Resolution." But if we believe in Surrender, that excuse is nonsense. Our lives will be one continuous daily surrender: surrender to God of every difficulty that confronts us, each temptation, each spiritual struggle, and laying them before our Higher Power either to take away or to show to us in their proper spiritual proportions. Continuous submission of our difficulties to God is not weakness, as some of us may imagine. Temptations to the world's spiritual leaders did and does not stop, nor are they less tempting than to us. None of us will ever be saints, but that is no reason why we should not be sensible spiritual travelers.

The Fellowship suggests our making the initial act of Surrender to God in the presence of another person who is already an active member, or if we choose, in the presence of a person who has for some time been a member of a religious body. In this wise advice lies the knowledge that a witness is a help to us to make our Surrender complete in the sight of God and humans; that like the oaths we take for mundane affairs, the witness's signature is often as valuable as our own.

The presence of a human witness should not be an embarrassment to us. Rather, it should be an outward sign of our intention to join a Fellowship of Surrendered lives among people, joining hands with that Fellowship at the same moment the direction of our lives goes out of our individual keeping into the hands of God. The Fellowship's initial act of Surrender is not in any way an outward and visible ceremony we feel we must shrink from. It is a simple decision put into simple language—spoken aloud to God, in front of another person, at any time and in any place—that we have decided to forget the past in God and to give our future into our Higher Power's keeping. Nothing more need be added; nothing can be taken away.

The Lord's Prayer is a perfect example of Surrender to God. In its composition, we are given in the shortest number of essential phrases the basics of our letting go to our Creator. If we have doubts about the Surrender to God that we use, we should say the Lord's Prayer to ourselves, dwelling on and thinking out the complete and absolute meaning of each word and phrase with direct application to ourselves. If we are busy people we can take only two or three minutes over each word or phrase. But we could continue to discover in this simple Prayer of Surrender limitless meanings and implications we never thought existed. It is a masterpiece among the most famous prayers of the world's religions that sums up who God is, where God is, God's attitude toward us, and what our attitude should be toward Our Higher Power.

The essential point in studying the Lord's Prayer as Surrender in its complete form is to ask ourselves if we really are convinced that we believe in and act on each phrase in our daily lives. To take the simplest example, do we believe absolutely that God is "Our Father" and we are *not God*— not only in the spiritual sense of the word but in our responsibilities to our Higher Power? If we are convinced of this, are we living our spiritual and material life based on those two words? Do we frankly acknowledge God as "Our Father" to the world? Or, because we are afraid of ridicule or not sure if its practical significance would work to our advantage in our daily lives, do we just treat it as two words in a prayer?

How many of us live our lives according to the simple logic that as God is "Our Father," we are all one family? Or do we say to ourselves: "That sounds excellent and idealistic on paper or at a meeting and we like to think it is true, but is it a possible working hypothesis?" How many of us realize that if we would believe and act on these two simple words, God's plan for us could come into action? Then the future, which is more serious than many newcomers can conceive in their beginning phase, would be assured for progressive happiness and contentment.

"Thy will be done" are the four little words that give us the crux to the surrender of our willpower—usually the last thing we wish to surrender to God. How many of us say daily to God, "Thy will be done—not mine. Thy Will shall be my will. I surrender to You that puny will of mine that I thought was my individual property and that, being of the earth, fails me when I most need it or causes me to lead a life of Self-worship"? Who among us can say that in Absolute Honesty, not only when we pray the Lord's Prayer but every time we come up against a problem in our lives?

Our Fellowship finds that desire and decision to make this Surrender do not come at any recognized or prearranged time in a life. Through a desire for recovery, effected by talks heard from other active members, some decide to surrender themselves quickly. Some, although wishing to make the change, take a prolonged time to come to a decision because they have honest doubts as to the definite necessity for that change in their life. Others are frankly mistrustful and doubt the Great Reality or are dubious of the effect a surrendered life may have on their immediate material, spiritual, mental, and physical existence.

The first impressions some people have of our suggested Program are anything but flattering. They mistrust the outspokenness of some members, dislike their direct methods of dealing with character defects, have criticisms that seem to them at the time to have foundations of truth. Some newcomers who go to meetings look for any reason they should not be there. Why? Mainly because they suspect other people of having faults they definitely have themselves, and because direct discussion of spiritual matters impels them immediately to look for ulterior motives. Sometimes when they fail to find these, they relapse. In some newcomers this attitude is natural. It is their spiritual disease, and that being what it is, it is not to be wondered at if they balk and engage in destructive criticism.

But these scoffers do not deter our Fellowship, whose message is for newcomers of all grades and kinds. It looks upon its critics in the only normal spiritual way—as excellent material for life changing. It is a remarkable fact that many of these scoffers, in spite of their ego-driven mistrust and suspicion, often return to meetings drawn—although they do not put it exactly like that—by a power stronger than themselves. And when they are Changed, as some of them eventually are, they become as progressive for the Group as they were formerly critical.

"I have learned, in whatever state I am, therein to be content," wrote Saint Paul.

We know from our experience that this is the state of life of those who are surrendered to God. It is the only contentment that withstands the urgings and promptings of the world toward the illusion of undue material gain and of those things that are ambitious for pomps and vanities. It is a balanced state, normal in outlook and in progression. There is nothing of fanaticism or fatalism about it. It is trust in the belief that whatsoever is good to us or a trial to us, whether it be joy or sorrow, plenty or little, love or hate, can be all turned to good account in God's service. And whatever God's will appoints to be best for us is the best we can choose for ourselves.

The state of contentment Saint Paul knew is not an idle or weak, effortless life in which we can sit back and do nothing. It is the result of an active spiritual life. To live fully is just as possible for us today as in Saint Paul's time. There is no one and nothing in this modern world, of which many of us are the discontented products, to prevent us from relinquishing our lives to God. Those of us who think there is put too much value on ourselves. To keep it from becoming more and more unbalanced, our world today needs more surrendered lives. Passive individuals are no more entitled to ignore the active spiritual fruits of their potential Surrender to God than they would be in keeping back any knowledge that would benefit their well-being.

None of us knows who are the key people in our future. The results of the Surrender of our lives may mean a change in others. We cannot predict what any single surrendered life is capable of accomplishing. Those who are doubting beginners only and who have not contemplated surrendering to God but have the problems of the world at heart, are ignoring, either through pride or self-worship, a practical opportunity to make a real contribution to their betterment. And those who are lazy members and cannot, because of lack of faith, use the abundance of power that God has put into their hands, are ignoring the fact that God can use everybody for the good of their fellow travelers. Even the most inarticulate or humble of us can assist God to work out to fruitful completion some little but important corner of God's plan.

S I N

(SHORTCOMINGS/ CHARACTER DEFECTS)

"*S*in," when put bluntly, "is anything that keeps us from God or from one another."

Sin is a word many people fight. To them the very word is out of date. It smacks of street-corner salvation meetings. They think only people who are behind the times believe in Sin these days. In their conversations it is seldom used, except, perhaps, to raise a laugh. But what colorful pictures Sin conjures up! Sin! When fashionable preachers call it scarlet and denounce the fashionable sins of their fashionable congregations in their fashionable churches, there is a thrill in Sin for some. They delight in going to hear their sins denounced. It is an entertainment well worth paying for! It gives them a feeling that to be denounced as wicked is a sign of social success. How very often are "The Sins of Mayfair" or "The Sins of Hollywood" the subjects of articles in the Sunday press, read with envious appreciation by the haves and have-nots.

Pathological psychology has become popular in recent years. Many suggest the subconscious be enthroned, like a mental giant that may rule our destiny and be at the root of all we think, do, or say. Any failing or abnormality, however hideous, can be blamed on our subconscious mind, which has

become a gold mine for those who seek to profit by the frailties of human nature.

Sin and temptation to Sin are called by any name but their
own. For many sins are repressed desires, inhibitions, fixations, morbid introspection, suppression of natural instincts—
anything but what they are—just plain Sin. We ask one of
these intelligent people, "Are you ever tempted to sin?" When
they reply, "Certainly not! But I have a suppressed desire to
shoplift," it is about as logical as an exercise in a French primer
that says, "Have you seen the pen of my aunt?" and replies,
"No, but my grandmother keeps bees."

Sin is a disease with consequences we cannot foretell or
judge; it is as contagious as any contagious disease our body
may suffer from. The sins we commit within this hour may have
unforeseen consequences even after we have long ceased to
draw living breath. That is not a morbid surmise; it is a truth.
None of us knows the future. Few of us know the consequences of even our simplest normal actions, so how can we
know where the direct or indirect effects of our negative behavior end?

Like physical disease, Sin needs antiseptics to prevent it
from spreading. Our spirit needs cleaning as much as the body
needs it. When what we call "conscience" pains us with remorse,
it is the spiritual equivalent to the pains our body sends us as
signals that it is disordered and needs attention.

Sin is a definite disorder of the soul. George Eliot has said:
"There is no sort of wrong deed of which a person can bear the
punishment alone; you can't isolate yourself and say that the
evil which is in you shall not spread. People's lives are as thoroughly blended with each other as the air they breathe; evil
spreads as necessarily as disease. Every sin causes suffering
to others beside those who commit it."

Unhappiness to us and others, discontent, and, frequently,
mental and bodily ill health are the direct results of our negative thinking or behavior. We need no science, deep study of
the power of thought, or psychoanalysis to make us realize that.

Negativity affects our general health. If we can be absolutely truthful to ourselves, we can analyze our wrongs for ourselves and trace their mental and physical effects. Negativity can dominate us mentally and physically until we are its abject slaves, just as we have been slaves to our active addiction. We cannot get rid of them by deciding to think no more about them. They *never* leave us of their own accord. Unless they are cut out by a decided surgical spiritual operation that will destroy them, roots and all, and begin to set us free from their killing obsession, they grow in time like a deadly moss within us until we become totally warped in outlook not only toward others but toward ourselves.

Some people think they are not sinners. If we were to ask them what their sins are, they would be unable to tell us because they would say they are not aware they have any. Nor, rack their brains though they might, could they quite understand what Sin means to them. These are the "nice" type of sinners who say they are not troubled by Sin. But if we were to ask them a few direct questions about their motives, outlook, or views on other people, if they are honest, they would see by what they think and say that Sin is a kind of pastime to them that they call being "natural" or "outspoken." The sins of "nice" people are often sins "nasty" people would despise themselves for, if they had them. We all know "nice" sinless sinners who need that surgical spiritual operation as keenly as the most miserable sinner of us all.

The Fellowship rightly believes that once we have shared our inventory with another person and surrendered our past wrongs to God, they are best forgotten. But some people cannot forget their sins even after they believe they have begun a new spiritual life. Listen to those who are Sin-conscious and cannot really relinquish their sins to God, and so get rid of them once and for all. How they delight in retelling their sins from which they have been "converted," although they refrain from admitting it, without at the same time making spiritual progress. How they cling to the glamour of their past exploits as if fascinated by them! They are not people with a Program but merely people with a past.

Pride in Sin, whether we say we are regenerated from it or whether we publish it to the world under the cloak of shame, is decided weakness some of us suffer from. When we decide to work and continue to make spiritual progress, our souls must be either clean or dirty; they cannot be both at the same time. Those of us who cannot get away from our past wrong-doing, in spite of thinking we are spiritually regenerated, have missed the point of Divine forgiveness, which is, in reality, plain cancellation.

True happiness is a life of recognizing and sharing our shortcomings and character defects, a life founded on trust in God, the life of right living. It is the happiness that attracts others to seek it because they see that the daily right attitude casts out fear of the past, the present, and the future.

No one makes sin but ourselves. Temptation is not action. It is an invitation we can accept or refuse. This invitation is often so worded or pictured in our mind that refusal seems beyond the power of our refusing. Because they are so often the most enjoyable part of sinning, in the same way that antic- ipation of a pleasurable event in life is often so much more enjoyable than the actual event itself, temptations are the allure of wrong doings and wrong thinking. If, as they come to us, we can give these invitations of Sin to God, our fellow members, sponsors, or friends for the answer, we have the certain knowledge that they will not be too strong for us to resist. Under the all-powerful light of our Higher Power, they shrink back into the darkness from whence they came.

In the "I" in the word *sin*, we are told, lies the secret of Sin's power. The "I" is our sick ego, and more important to many than spiritual health. All we do contrary to our simple program is traceable to it. If we can suddenly, slowly, or grad- ually surrender that "I" to God, Sin goes with it. When we live by reducing daily that "I" in our lives we have fewer prob- lems. "I" is a little letter with big responsibilities. It is the one letter in the alphabet that has a personality.

Every time we try to move forward spiritually, that "I" confronts us. It is the fence we put up to separate our very own part of existence from that of other people's, when we want to think we are so very different from everybody else. "I'm sure you can't understand that I am not the same as other people," we say. "I am so very different. I have a good excuse for doing what I did. I know it's no use my explaining to you. But I know what I am. I . . . I . . . I . . . " And so the "I" in that little word Sin dominates us, making us feel that our "I" is tremendously important in the scheme of things. While all the time it means that we are looking only at ourselves and are completely oblivious of God.

Individual self-interest is the primary cause of wrong doings. The Fellowship's vision of individuals set free from the destroying influence of active addiction and their character defects and shortcomings is not vague idealism. It is a definitely possible spiritual realization that can be brought about by *practicing these principles* and making progress according to our suggested Program.

SHARING FOR CONFESSION

*S*haring our inventories as practiced by the Group is sharing in the ordinary sense of the word. In plain language it is telling, or talking over, our defects with another whose life has already been surrendered to God. Or, if we have already surrendered, it is assisting others to surrender—as we are guided—by openly laying our past mistakes or present temptations alongside theirs, so that they may be better able to recognize and bring to light those obstacles that have stood between them and God.

Sharing on this basis, in practice as well as in theory, is not only good fellowship but also sound psychologically. "Two minds are better than one" is an old saying that is more true when the subject in discussion is common to both parties, and Sin is certainly common to everybody. Sharing—call it "mutual confession" if you wish—is not a new idea recently devised by an emotional mind, but rather one of the rudiments of simple Christianity long since gone out of practice, except in certain faiths that have retained Confession to God via a priest. The sacrament of Penance for many people is a useful and excellent disciplinary religious act.

"Get it off your chest and you'll feel better" is wise advice from a wise friend to those of us who are troubled by life and feel that if we are Sin-obsessed any longer, we shall lose our faith in humanity as well as in ourselves. Mental healers, whether they be secular or religious, recognize the value of our "getting it off our chests." Their treatment cannot be efficacious nor their understanding of our symptoms complete if we cannot do that thoroughly. Of recent years mental doctoring of all kinds and guises has become popular, often reviving as new scientific discoveries old truths based on a simple understanding of human nature. These metaphysical or psychopathologic doctors or healers have taken these old truths and adapted them to modern requirements—sometimes with excellent results, sometimes destroying where they have no power to rebuild. Simple sins are often treated by these mental practitioners as inhibitions, and human temptations as mental disorders, and it is not surprising that when these have been removed, they immediately open doors to others, sometimes of a worse type.

A medical practitioner can only do us real good when we are physically ill if, either by asking us or by their own deductions, they find out the exact nature of our illness and then endeavor to put health in the place of our sickness. Character defects are symptoms of spiritual sickness. Telling our moral inventory to another, as we would tell our physical symptoms to a doctor, enables us not only to understand our spiritual sickness but also to find out how to take out a new lease on spiritual health.

No one will ever realize to what extent God can work through the spiritual to remove the troubles of the mental and physical. It is only known that God can give limitless power of resistance to any condition that is caused by negative thinking and behavior. Setting the mind free through truth can work mental and physical wonders.

Sins are weeds that flourish and choke. If we alone cannot pull them out of our own gardens, we must have someone to do the weeding for us, to help us burn them on the rubbish heap. Then, after we have set fire to them, we can turn our backs on them and walk away toward a new life. Sharing our inventory brings the sins into the open light, giving them their proper spiritual status, listing them according to their importance to us, making us acknowledge their existence. We deny them no longer as they become hard facts to be faced squarely and in due time removed by God's help. No one is sinless; that is the common ground for sharing.

"Confess your sins one to another, and pray one for another, that you may be healed." To some of us that sounds very easy on paper but difficult or almost impossible in actual practice. "How could I confess everything—my moral inventory—even to someone who knows me very well? I have sins my closest friends do not suspect my having. Why, I couldn't even put them into words!" How many of us think like that! We maintain a strange delusion that we are special people and that our sins are so very original. We really believe that if we do admit to another, they would open their eyes wide and look at us as if we had taken leave of our senses.

But if we talk over our list with anyone whose life is God-Directed, our wrongs are not flattering to our belief of their originality. The surprising and healthy discovery we make in Sharing is that all our sins are also the sins of others. This discovery lifts from us the feeling of isolation and despair of Self. We find we can give our sins into another's and God's keeping with as much relief as we would discard a heavy winter coat on a hot summer's day. The cooling breeze of God-given reason goes through our soul, mind, and body, and we rejoice in new-found freedom and exultant hope in the future.

The discovery that our wrongs are often the sins of our neighbor gives a particularly healthy outlook to the young. Suicides by young people attributable to temporary insanity are often caused by the feeling that there is no escape from sins they believe peculiar to themselves. The agony of the young mind is indescribable when obsessed and warped by natural sins of the body. These sins could easily be placed on a normal basis for eradication by an understanding talk with one who has been through that agony and by God's help emerged a free human being. Youthful sins in time often become harmful, fixed habits with a resulting bad inferiority complex. The average adolescent mind is a delicate structure, impressionable, eager for adventure, timorous of criticism, reaching out toward the glamorous climax of full experience, to enjoy the fruition of the urgent desires that must surge up as the body develops.

Parents Sharing with a child the knowledge that they, too,

went through the phase that their child now finds so torturous to his or her physical and spiritual outlook; an older member Sharing with a newcomer; a friend with a friend; these can lay simply and easily those ghosts that have haunted them.

"Pray one for another." What sound advice we can find in that simple instruction for all our difficulties! In Sharing it is no less of real aid than at any other time, for it is taking another's burden, putting it into words, and placing it before God. The consciousness that another human being will pray to God that our troubles be taken from us and ask this of God with as much urgency and sincerity as if those short-comings were our own is one of the most beautiful and real qualities of our Fellowship. To those of us who have never had this experience, a new and unforgettable spiritual discovery is in store.

The Fellowship, realizing the use of the Sharing of sins, tells us that it is possible that we may be healed. In fact it is as essential as before Surrendering our lives to God so that our spiritual selves are healed of our soul's sickness.

To those of us—and there are many—who need God-Guided counsel, Sharing is not only a necessity but a distinct blessing. The Fellowship of other men and women—who know how difficult it is for us to believe our sins are forgiven us, and who know that putting our wrongs and spiritual problems into words to another—helps us in becoming honest with God. Sharing does not mean that we have to go up or down to another person's level. It is not patronage or superiority on either side. It is two people having a common interest—character defects—and getting a healthy viewpoint on them.

"Why shouldn't I go straight to God if I want to admit my wrongs? Why should I bother about another person inter-fering? The right and only person for my confession is God." Some people, when this part of our Program is explained to them, say this, and often with indignation. It is a natural point of view to many. It would be perhaps unkind of us to ask them if they do admit to God, and how much they admit—and how much they keep back. We can, however, tell them that we do not deny that they can go straight to God if they wish and God will forgive them. But if they wish for a sure and certain knowledge that their past sins—and all of them—are to be wiped out, once and for all, this moral inventory must be brought into the open and honestly faced. To put them into words, before God, with another person as a witness, is the only healthy way of making sure that the spiritual system is cleansed.

To pretend that everybody needs to Share in order to live a spiritual life would be idle of us. None of us can judge how another stands with God. But few spiritually centered people refuse Sharing on the plea of confessing directly to God, because that person would realize that by talking over with a sin-burdened soul their own difficulties, he or she would be able to bring that soul into communion with God.

Sharing in no way trespasses on or takes the place of Confession before a priest, should this Confession be part of any of our faith. The Group, working within the Churches, does not in any way claim that Sharing in the sense of confession is their spiritual prerogative or their religious invention. They definitely recognize that Sharing is an invaluable aid to reclaiming lives for God. They recognize that the nominal faith of the person is not of so much importance as that the person, after being Changed, can return to his or her faith, become a spiritually alive member of it, and be able to use its teachings with a new understanding and renewed spiritual vitality. There is no religion with all of its flock inside its teachings. Nor is there any religion that would not welcome back stray sheep, however dubious "orthodoxy" might think the shepherd's means are to bring it back to the fold again.

Sharing does not mean divulging indiscretions that involve naming other people. It means confessing our part in our sinning. Placing the blame on others and making excuses for our weaknesses is not Sharing; it is merely negative, selfish talk. On the other hand, some of us find it hard not to let exhibitionism in a mild form enter everything we do concerning ourselves. We always want to be thought clever and important even when we talk about our sins. We can hardly resist painting our sins in bright colors and making ourselves heroes and heroines of the great spiritual conflicts we have fought, although we may have succumbed to Sin in the fight. Pride is a cunning foe. It can enter even our accusations against ourselves, giving us a stimulating enjoyment and ego boost from our confessions, although we may not acknowledge it.

Confessions shared become the property of God, not other people. Every active member with time in the Program recognizes this, and newcomers should have no fear that such frankness will become the property of others. Our private lives remain our private lives. The past is with God; we have only the future before us.

Our common sense will prevent us from having qualms about which person we Share with. On occasion, all of us meet those who complement our own nature, those we feel instinctively will "understand" or have passed through the very phase we are passing through and with whom we know telling our life story will remain secret from other people. Those are the people in whom we should confide our spiritual difficulties.

Sharing is not a question of sympathy. The less sympathy, as mere sympathy, and the more common sense, spiritual assistance, and God-given understanding there is in it, the better for us.

Some of us wallow in our remorse. It is only with great difficulty that we can refrain—if we refrain—from Sharing our sins with anyone, anywhere, at any time. This is the old foolish self, which will not lie down and succumb in proper decency. It is a form of self-advertisement that no life knows in the least degree if it has, in truth, been changed to God. It is therefore essential that we should make perfectly certain that our confessions once shared and forgiven are forgotten, except when we bring them out as dead specimens in our stores to show what the Fellowship has done for us.

In all our lives, we know and meet people who would be happier and freer if they were not weighed down with Sin. They are the charge of all active Group members. They are the God-given opportunity for us to be able to make them say with the author of Hebrews: "Therefore let us also, seeing we are all compassed about with so great a cloud of witnesses, lay aside every weight, and the sin which does so easily beset us, and let us run with patience the race that is set before us."

WITNESS

(S T O R Y)

*T*he Fellowship is Witness for a new way of life—an Ambassador conveying goodwill to all people in a world in which goodwill is conspicuous by its absence. Its assets are a belief in the existence of a living Higher Power and proof of God's forgiveness. These are not assets that make a person rich in worldly goods or assured of a life of comfort.

But responsible the world over, we go on with our work to bring others to our Program with honesty and conviction of what God has done for us since we have surrendered to a life of spiritual truth.

Witness is Sharing with others the main reasons and the concrete results of our surrender to God. Just talking spirituality and all it should mean to others is of little use when the world talks too much already. Faith without works is dead. In itself, the Fellowship's joy in living and working makes evident by example better than any words could do. It uses the power of the Fellowship of the Spirit to change other people's lives.

God's disclosure shows the best way of approach, when to share from our own lives, and when and how to help others. We must not forget for a moment that we all are human, have temptations as strong as others and, but for the grace of God, would still be unhappy in our soul. Our simplicity and directness to help is better than the finest rhetoric or logical arguments.

Personal proof of experience can do more than the best of theories. Personal experiences tell of what we know as a positive truth. Generalization and guesswork are not in our Program. It is not surprising, therefore, that we are rapidly rekindling the fire of living universal spiritual truth. The quickening glow from it is making people, even in far-off lands, wonder at this revitalizing challenge that is being issued to the world.

People in need are more inclined to tell us the truth about themselves if they know we are telling them the truth about ourselves. This is the foundation of the mutual trust that is essential when we share our experience to help others. In families, this mutual trust is invaluable in that it enables barriers of age and different personalities to be broken down so all can work their own Program. Members of families whose tastes differ often find the serious mention of God by one of their number rather an awkward topic.

Talking to our family and relatives is often more difficult than sharing with friends or acquaintances. In modern homes they would say that "it is hardly the thing to do" because it embarrasses them. But, given trust in the member's sincerity and the definite proof of God's influence in the member's life, the possibilities of one family member changing the whole are infinite. This the Fellowship has proved.

We can all be living proof of the power of the Program, all of us who are examples of what the Fellowship has done for us. We have a message to give the world. Our message must not only be of hope but also of concrete example. It means telling others of our own past experiences, of our Surrender, and after, of the power of the God of our understanding in our lives and the spiritual strength given us to overcome our present difficulties. We have to remember that it is our convictions that will convince other people, that half measures will be as fruitless as no measures at all. Our honesty will invite honesty from others. Nothing else will.

When we were newcomers, we remembered what Sharing

meant to us when we were tired of ourselves, tired of problems against which we felt helpless, tired of continually repeating the same mistakes, and tired of living. In Sharing we understand what George Meredith meant when he wrote: "We drank the pure daylight of honest speech."

RESTITUTION

(A M E N D S)

*I*n these days we moderns believe tremendously more in what we see than in what we hear. We want concrete facts, not theories. There is no time to dally with fine-sounding idealisms or to spend much of what we believe is "precious" time listening to long sermons, as did our fore-bears. We want action—action with immediate results that are obvious to everybody. Modern reason and doubt are influenced by the material. "Show us!" is our cry. Everything comes under that demand. We want results about the spiritual as well as the material. We must be convinced.

"Wisdom is the principal thing; therefore get wisdom: yes, with all you have gotten, get understanding," we are told in Proverbs. We believe it is of little use for us to get the wisdom of what God's power and will can mean in our lives, to Surrender to our Higher Power and attempt to live changed lives. If that wisdom does not show us that it is absolutely essential that we should get understanding with those we love, work with, or come in contact with in our daily lives. We cannot get that understanding with them unless we are honest about our wrong thoughts and actions in connection with them.

Restitution is openly cutting the cord of sin that has bound us to the life of wrong we have lived in the past. The only way of doing this is by acknowledging our faults to the people concerned and to pay back by apology, or in kind if necessary, that which we have taken from them. Whatever it is, important or seemingly unimportant, we are debtors and must pay now that our lives are God's. It is definitely not only a question of "owning up" but also confirming the cancellation of the debt we owe of making concrete restitution.

Restitution is righting to the best of our present ability wrongs we have committed in the past. The reception given to our acts of restitution by those to whom we make them is in itself an interesting sidelight on human character. Often because we are honest and frankly acknowledge a mistake to the person we have wronged, that person is awakened to the realization of what a Changed Life may mean to him or her. And our act of restitution not only brings forgiveness with it but also a new life to God. Only ill-timed atonement might cause harm. But nearly always in making amends by sheer honesty, it brings us new friends or a better understanding with our old friends. The honesty of restitution is usually a new wonder to those who have been unaware until then of what a surrendered life can mean, in a world where dishonesty is often taken for granted and truth has lost much of its meaning.

To strangers of our Fellowship, Changed Lives, unless they have something concrete to show for that change, are not in themselves evidence of spiritual reawakening. And in these days to make people who doubt sit up and take notice of anything that is not entirely of the earth, changed people must be concrete. Changed ways of living, changed outlook, and changed attitude toward others are essential for our new Way of Life. Restitution is the one thing that often causes unchanged people to rub their eyes and wonder if a new phenomenon, the exact nature of which they cannot define, has come into their world, making them feel either that the universe is growing even madder or that it is becoming very sane.

Confronted by a Changed person who comes to make restitution for some wrong done, many people are not sure how to deal with the situation. Seemingly out of the blue, someone comes with honesty and humility to make restitution for a wrong done to them! It is unprecedented. There are no printed rules or regulations they can refer to that will tell them how to deal with this strange situation without loss of dignity or acquiring patronage. And more important than that, there is obviously no ulterior motive in the amazing visit of this person who has come to them voluntarily to confess, ask forgiveness, and, if the wrong demands it, to repay. That, in itself, is unique and is not to be dealt with by reference to any book of words.

As they listen to this individual who suddenly confronts them, these strangers to restitution often do not understand the feelings they experience. Yes, the world, they are quite certain, is becoming very mad—or, perhaps, very, very sane!

They would be surprised, these people, if the Fellowship told them that, when confronted with a Changed Life making restitution to them, their mixed feelings are due not to men or women talking about wrong and right but to the unusual situation of one's soul facing another with Absolute Honesty and with God as witness. There is little wonder that from a worldly point of view, restitution appears as a phenomenon. More often than not, those people utter no words of condemnation or of ridicule, for often during our restitution to others God often speaks to them about themselves.

Those who have surrendered and made complete amends for their wrongs to other people are in agreement that they have never regretted making the right sort of restitution, whatever the cost has been to them. It often requires more courage than some of us can imagine ourselves possessing to make an amend that might conceivably spell ruin in the eyes of society. But, those who wish to put themselves right with God know they must also put themselves right with people. And so a person tells another a fault that has been the cause of their drifting apart. A confession goes to someone too far off to own up to by spoken word and atones for a wrong. An employer is interviewed by an employee who acknowledges some wrong done against him and vice versa. Mistakes are acknowledged, forgiveness asked. But whatever the occasion of the restitution, it is not just an empty dramatic gesture with no true or constructive significance. It is an indispensable condition for the birth of a new spiritual life.

Restitution is not easy. Only those who have done so realize the strength sometimes needed to write even a letter of amends to a person thousands of miles away to set right a wrong even though that wrong may be known only to the writer. It may be a mistake that might never come to light but for the letter of restitution, or a mistake that appears trivial to the world. Perhaps we have been dishonest or uncharitable only in thought. But, without God's positive power behind us, a letter about what may seem to strangers a trivial matter but one that will get us right with ourselves and others is often difficult even to place in the mail.

So we stand wondering about the possible effects of slipping that letter in that mailbox and allowing it to fall where we can never retrieve it. Doubting God, a wave of self-consciousness comes over us, a feeling that we may be making fools of ourselves unnecessarily, lowering our prestige, asking for trouble. We feel a conviction that the unconfessed past is the past and is best forgotten. But while we hesitate, if we realize that God is really with us and that an act of restitution, great or small as it may be, is necessary, our hand, God-Guided, without hesitation creeps up to the mailbox, and the letter goes beyond our recalling, to carry out one more demonstration of goodwill that will set us free from our past selves.

Ancient wisdom suggests: "And pour contempt on all my pride"! That is one of the secrets not only of restitution but of a spiritual life. What great unimaginable possibilities it conjures up for us! If we could pour contempt on all our pride, no avenue of spiritual life would be closed to us. There is nothing we would hesitate to do to put ourselves right with God and people. Self would go by the board, and in its place a great understanding would come. Restitution would be the perfect

God-Guided act for our spiritual progress, not only when we initially change our lives to the Higher Power of our understanding, but throughout the challenges of our striving for a spiritual life. How many of us can pour contempt on all our pride—not 50 percent, but 100 percent of it? Or how many realize what that contempt would mean to us? It would not be just ignoring our pride but spurning it as if it were something far too inferior to our nature to be noticed.

"When Pride comes, then comes Shame," is what the proverb says. Pride enters into many more things that we think, say, or do than we realize. Even when we make restitution, pride tries hard to take a hand. "Shall I bother to tell the authorities that I did something that was the cause of So-and-So getting into trouble, although he was innocent?" says a person contemplating restitution. "If I confess now it may mean losing all my friends, having to leave the town, being laughed at for raking up a silly scandal that died down years ago. It may mean being made to feel small and ridiculous for not leaving well alone. Anyway, if I do confess, I feel I shall never be able to lift up my head again." And so pride goes on, giving us what appear to be good excuses for not making atonement for some wrongs that lie hidden from others, but not from God. If we could only be honest with ourselves and pour contempt on all our pride, we should realize that this very act of restitution is absolutely necessary, whatever the cost, if we are to right an injustice to another and put ourselves right with God.

"What if my restitution toward a certain person does more harm than good?" Some of us, with good reason, ask that. The answer is that where it is essential, the important thing for us is to go through with restitution, for none of us knows for certain what effect our acts of making amends will have until we have made them. The results of restitution are often so unexpectedly in our favor that we wonder afterward why we had any qualms about making it.

Into this problem there enters the important solution of

God-Guidance. It is the acid test of the good and the wisdom of our intentions and the arbitrator for our decisions. If we remember that surrendered lives are in truth God-Directed lives and that we have the purity of right living as our example, prayer can help us where we cannot help ourselves. We are often inclined to forget that God can take care of other people as well as us.

Spiritual discretion is often the better part of mental valor when we contemplate making restitution. It is of no profit to God or others for us to wreck innocent lives by indiscretions prompted by overzeal. God-given guidance should prompt all our acts of restitution, telling us what atonement constitutes, the right time to make it, the form it should take. If we need it, guidance will give the spiritual strength to carry it out for the best of all parties concerned. There is no knowing the great good our courage will do if it is really God-Guided. We may never know how many lives may be improved because of it or what it may mean in spiritual gain to us.

In the Parable of the Prodigal Son, we are given the classic example of restitution. It is always worth repeating. The Prodigal Son says,

> *I will arise and go to my father, and will say unto him "Father, I have sinned against heaven, and in thy sight: I am no more worthy to be called thy son: make me as one of thy hired servants." And he arose, and came to his father. But while he was yet afar off, his father saw him and was moved with compassion, and ran, and fell on his neck, and kissed him.*
>
> *And the son said unto him, "Father, I have sinned against heaven, and in thy sight: I am no more worthy to be called thy son."*
>
> *But the father said to his servants, "Bring forth quickly the best robe, and put it on him; and put a ring on his hand, and shoes on his feet: and bring the fatted calf, and kill it; and let us eat, and make merry: for this my son was dead, and is alive again; he was lost, and is found."*

Such is the Divine conception of the act of restitution. There we have in the last sentence the true definition of a changed life. "[He] was dead, and is alive again . . . was lost, and is found."

That pride does not enter in this perfect example of making amends is obvious to us. The son makes no excuses for his errors. He shoulders them and faces his father; he is simple, direct, and honest. That is exactly what our restitution should be, although it may be misunderstood by those who hear the rejoicing but do not know the cause. God shows us that some people are unable to comprehend restitution and forgiveness. In the parable the elder son, who has heard his father's rejoicing at the younger son's return, complains to his father, reminding him of his good service that has received no such reward. The father replies to the elder son's protests by again saying: "For this my son was dead, and is alive again; he was lost, and is found." That is the perfect description of a changed life. It is inevitable that unless we can make others understand all that restitution means to a changed life people of the elder-son type always will be with us.

We must not expect all our acts of restitution to be received with acclamations of joy, as if we are all prodigal sons returning home and should therefore receive the modern equivalent of a fatted calf. Our amends may perhaps mean payment that will be a trial to us, or they may be flatly ignored. But if we make our restitution in the right spirit it is certain that we shall know that our Higher Power is an inward reality.

GUIDANCE

(C O N S C I O U S   C O N T A C T)

*D*ivine guidance to a life changed from self to spiritual principles is taking normal intelligence and directing it in the fullest harmony with God's will for the good of the individual and the individual's neighbors.

Seeming trivialities are not overlooked by our Higher Power. A small point overlooked today may have a big consequence tomorrow. Suggestions as to conduct or solutions to material and spiritual difficulties are given by daily conscious contact. It is God in partnership with us, using for our best the lives we have surrendered to our individual Higher Power's care.

We realize that guidance is not anyone's particular property. It is as free to all of us as are the sun and air. There is no reason why everyone, whatever their status or spiritual belief, cannot come out of the darkness to breathe the clear and spiritual health-giving properties of God's radiant counsel. "Every good gift and every perfect boon is from above." Improvement of our conscious contact takes on eventful potentialities, is full of interest, and is in accordance with every type of personality. It is all wise and all embracing, building up our right God-appointed kind of ego, until we feel that life in the future will always be for us that adventurous feeling of youth and hope that is reborn within most of us when we breathe the exhilarating air of Spring on a glorious, fresh morning.

Conscious contact takes away from us that fear of tomorrow that, in conjunction with the troubles of today, so often makes life intolerable for us. Not only is our today in God's keeping but also our tomorrow, surrendered to our Higher Power. Why fear whatever we think tomorrow must bring us as a logical consequence of today's events? Fear of the future, whether it be tomorrow or old age, means that we do not trust in God's will for us.

Our faith in the future is the maximum test of our faith in God. How many people have it? Can we visualize half the world or even our few friends free from fear not only of the present but also of the future? If this could be, unbalanced civilization would slow down to its proper course, like a stream that has battled its way through rocks and crevices and reached, at long last, a smooth, straight course, where the sunlight ripples through its crystal clearness, as it flows serenely on to meet the Great Ocean of the Spirit.

A Quiet Time (prayer and meditation) with our Higher Power every morning before "the daily toil and common round" of the world commences will put us in the right key for the day. These early morning Quiet Times in which God impresses on our minds wisdom which becomes living spots in the routine of ordinary life. Many of us use a pencil and notebook so that we may record every God-given thought and idea that comes to us during our time alone with our Higher Power. This way, no detail, however small, may be lost to us, and we may not shirk the truth about ourselves or any problem, when it comes to us.

It is not suggested that everything we write down during our Quiet Times necessarily comes from God. The human mind, being what it is, wanders from concentration at an outside interruption, takes up a train of thought it finds hard to discard, invents or remembers a thought of its own. But to those closely in touch with God to differentiate between spiritual and human messages becomes progressively easier. In cases of difficulty our guidance can be "checked up" with the teachings of many good books or by conference with others who are also receiving guidance in Quiet Times.

Prayer is the natural complement of God-Direction. We cannot expect God to talk to us if we do not talk to God, but it is not always essential to ask God continually for help in every move we make, or in every problem of our daily lives. If we have faithfully surrendered our lives to a Higher Power, God is our Pilot and knows our every movement and thought. When we listen for God's guidance during our Quiet Times all requests asked or unasked are answered. Petitions are not always necessary, for if our attitude toward God is conducive to real guidance, then that in itself is prayer.

The age of miracles is still with us, although we may not see the signs in the sky or the spectacular manifestations on earth that we may think miracles are. Real prayer receives a real answer in any place, at any time. "God works in a mysterious way His wonders to perform" in a world that confuses the material shadow with the spiritual substance. No request to God from the heart is ever lost. We may think the answer to it is a long time coming or that it is not answered in the way we want. But to God, who knows neither Space nor Time, it is the best answer at the best time for us.

Words in every language, spoken aloud or mentally formed, in sincere prayer are active spiritual messages radiating to God and received by our Higher Power as soon as they are uttered. Prayer does not depend on an attitude of the physical body but on the attitude of the spiritual self. Neither does prayer, of necessity, bring a feeling of spiritual elevation, nor does its reality depend on the form or the wording our petitions take. Fixed forms of prayer used in services are necessary for united worship, and written prayers emanating from God-fearing men and women are real aids to our closer communion with God. But neither a Church nor a saintly composer of the most beautiful prayer would suggest that the fixed prayer is more than a guide to the prayer we should pray when we are alone with God.

It is necessary in our Quiet Times to give our minds to God free from doubts and distractions, to ensure our absolute negation to everything but our conviction that God can, and will, tell us what our Higher Power thinks best for us to do, or not to do, in the plan of our daily lives, or in a problem that confronts us. If we truly believe our guidance is from God, we must recognize that to ask God numberless times for help in a difficulty is not necessary.

With real human insight, the Reverend R. H. Steuart, in his helpful little essay *A Map of Prayer*, gets down to the difficulties the average person has in shutting himself or herself entirely away from the world when in prayer. He writes,

> *Distractions may be divided roughly into two kinds: Thoughts about one's daily activities, past, present, and future; associations called up by sounds and movements around us; definite temptations of every description, coming from one knows not where. Weariness, with accompanying disgust for our present occupation; doubts about the prayer itself, fears of idleness, self-delusion, vanity; strong impulses to get up at once and do something else—this, often, just when our sensible devotion is at its strongest. These are often, too, intensified by secret doubts about the forgiveness of past mistakes, and clouded by an indefinable feeling that somehow I am radically different, for the worse, from every one else, and that, do what I may, I never shall and never can get nearer to God.*

Prayer and Quiet Times with God are similar in the various distractions and doubts that often beset them. When a God-thought comes into our mind we sometimes doubt its authenticity. We say to ourselves, "It's all very well to get that as guidance, but what is the use of it to me without the practical means to carry it out?" It is then that we are forgetting that God never guides us to do anything without the means to carry that out. "Faith is the assurance of things hoped for, the proving of things not seen." If we trust and go right ahead to carry out God's instructions, however obscure the means or objective may seem to us, it is amazing to the unenlightened mind how God not only provides the guidance but the assistance and the outcome that is best for us according to God's plan.

Doubt stifles and makes difficult our attempt to act upon God-Counsel. When we fearlessly carry out God-given prompting to do what may seem at the moment impossible in our circumstances, we see the example from the Christian religion the Divine meaning and implication of Christ's walking on the water—for all time. Christ walked on the water to show everyone that by faith everything is possible. He walked that water trusting in God. It was Christ's demonstration to all people of the power of Faith. "According to our faith is it possible unto us," was Christ's message.

Self-will is the hardest thing in existence to surrender to God. The majority of us will surrender just enough of ourselves to our Higher Power so that we can keep what we think is our independence. It is that little piece of self-will we keep, even though we think it is so secret and hidden that our Higher Power will not notice it. This prevents us from receiving the infinite and complete benefits and grace of guidance.

We must give our entirety to God in our Quiet Times and when we are carrying God's guidance out. This seems at first as difficult as is giving one's entire thoughts and concentration to God in prayer. But discipline over our self-will, although it may be slow, comes with practice. And practice and regularity are as necessary to learning to make the best use of prayer and meditation as they are in learning anything that is worth learning in this world.

THE FOUR ABSOLUTES

ABSOLUTE HONESTY

"To thine own self be true," said Shakespeare, "and it must follow as the night the day you can't then be false to any man." Give to ourselves the absolute truth, be to others as truthful as we are to ourselves. Can we do it? Can we sit down even for a few moments and face the self the world does not see and tell that self the absolute truth? Then, having told that hidden self the absolute truth, can we be honest and let that truth become a conscious part of ourselves? How many of us can do that?

Absolute honesty is the proud boast of many people. "One thing about me," they will say, "is that no one can deny that I'm always honest about everything and everybody." We all know that complacent type too well. They enjoy taking inventory of other people's weaknesses and indiscretions to their face and are rather surprised when the recipients of this form of honesty are not exactly pleased. Why on earth should other people be pleased when we destroy their illusions or lay bare their weak points? The methods of the self-righteous, who would be honest at all costs but their own, are more harmful to spiritual life than they realize.

Under God's guidance, absolute truthfulness is tempered with common sense and kindliness. There is no reason why we should flaunt and enjoy what we think is Absolute Honesty so much that we should tell a neighbor a truth about themselves that is neither a shortcoming of theirs nor our business. Striving for Absolute Honesty should not be a weapon for us to bludgeon our way to what we think is perfection. "Love your neighbor as yourself" is sufficient test as to our motives for honesty.

There is no reason why, in our determination to be honest with God, we should destroy the belief in God in other people. Many people's belief in God is founded on their belief in humanity, kindliness, faithfulness, in the fulfillment of obligations, moral or material. God-given discretion is better than our unloving determination to be honest at all costs, mostly other people's.

"An honest man's the noblest work of God," quotes Robert Burns. Honesty must be allied to nobility of mind and purpose. Some of us use frankness as a sort of scourge to punish those we feel are not quite as good as we think we are. Minds such as these are farther from their Higher Power's than they suppose. Honesty is the truth that belongs to God, and when we use it we are using God's power. If we use God's power in the wrong way or at the wrong time, why should we grumble because it is ineffective or has the opposite effect to what we think it should have? A sudden fit of frankness about other people without a preliminary self-inventory can do untold harm. We must be absolutely honest with ourselves before we can be absolutely honest about other people. It is one of the essentials of our new way of life.

Many people revel in what they think is Absolute Honesty. They are convinced that it means telling the bald, unvarnished facts about themselves even if it involves other people. If the truth is without consideration or discretion, then to keep a silent tongue and await the decision of our guidance is better than to blurt out what may be a truth, but a truth that will harm someone. God-given counsel is wise counsel. Petty criticisms do not induce a vital faith in God. Truth should not be merely destructive but spiritually constructive. Honesty is not, of necessity, criticism. If Love is the rock from which our fountain of Honesty springs, then it is Honesty in its purest sense.

Family life must have its roots in honesty if the family is to remain united. It is not surprising that children who know that their parents are not honest with each other are not honest with their parents. Modern children are said by some popular writers to be an unsolvable problem, a kind of phenomenon in the social history of the world. Children of any age are a problem to the grownups of a previous generation, and they always will be. Modern children are products of modern conditions, and as they grow with it they have to adapt themselves to the changing conditions of the world.

It is not the fault of the modern children that a large percentage of them are happy-go-lucky nonbelievers who have discarded God as an out-of-date institution. Their eyes are naturally eagerly fixed on the promised fruits of life, vitality, and progress. If their parents or their teachers cannot, or will not, show the power of honesty to youth as a living force that does not bind youth but offers it the best and fullest way of living, then the fault is theirs. Youth will not face the undeniable truth that the simple rules of all ancient faiths are as modern and as applicable to enjoyment and appreciation of life as its best today.

Honesty in right moral conduct is essential to a real happiness that has no fear of the present or the future. How can any relationship live in perfect understanding if either has a secret that, should it come to light from an outside source, will wreck their partnership? If real, unshakable love exists between two people, whatever the fault that one may confess to the other, it will sink into insignificance, or take its proper place between them, if honesty is made as a tribute to that love.

Reluctance to be honest about our faults or mistakes with a person we are united to by love is lack of faith, not only in that person but also in the reality of that love. A love is not worth having that dies because with honest motives, one confesses a problem to the other. Any love that can embrace mutual honesty is near to the ideal that God has for men and women.

Moral honesty with our friends, who cooperate with us for happiness, is necessary if we are to know that we can rely on them to stand with us in an emergency. How much more do we value friends whose affection is founded on candor and who will be honest with us when we are confronted with difficult situations in which we need honesty if we are to set a right viewpoint? What are the use of half-truths, empty words of consolation, or negative advice to us when we are facing a crisis that needs to be confronted with Absolute Honesty?

Some of us are like the proverbial ostrich, which hides its head in the sand. How often do we say, "If it's anything unpleasant I don't want to hear it!" when subconsciously we know that the best thing for us would be to face the truth honestly and seek for an honest solution to our problem or our shortcoming. We cannot always hide our heads in the sands with the fallacy that ignorance is bliss. Our heads have to come out sometimes, and we often find that while we have been shutting our eyes to it, the truth has grown much more difficult to cope with. Friendship that will allow for honest facing of mutual difficulties is the only kind of friendship that is worth our having. The mutual ostrich kind is hardly friendship; it certainly is not honest.

How anyone can possibly be even apparently honest in these days is a question that is very natural. In business today, which for most people is one big fight for bare existence, let alone profit, honesty has often become forgotten. Cutthroat competition, false trading representations, underhanded methods of selling, or lack of capital worry thousands into premature old age and disillusion. "Do others before they can do you" is often the motto of the modern business world. But does it bring lasting fruits to anyone? Millionaires' wealth increases even while they sleep. But some millionaires are never free, can call five minutes of the waking day their own, or can have one really free minute alone to face God, to whom money is only the invention of Humans and who recognizes the accumulation of wealth by people as the mirage it is.

How many people who worship money only crash every year from their gilded heights to depths the average person is spared from? Many of us feel we want to be millionaires, and in some aspects it is an understandable ambition. But for every million added to the wealth of one person, a million is gained from countless others. The natural wealth of the world is neither ours nor theirs; it is God's. We are all stewards to our Higher Power for God's property, by God's permission. That is a fact no spiritual reality can refute.

As that is so, why should we be so ridiculous as to think we can prosper to any real happiness if we use dishonest methods to gain undue possession of the wealth that at its source is Absolute Honesty? The popular belief is that honesty cannot go hand in hand with business. But it can. Many of our Fellowship who are in business have witnessed that honesty makes not only for the right kind of business with a just profit, but also gains them friends. Any astute business person knows that a friend in the business world is a considerable asset. Being honest in business does not mean being a fool. "Render therefore unto Caesar the things that are Caesar's; and unto God the things that are God's," said the prophet. Absolute Honesty in business means our being level, our playing the game of business as cleanly as we would play any other game.

"Whatsoever ye do, work heartily, as unto the Lord, and not unto men," said the Christian writer Saint Paul. Whatever our work in life, Absolute Honesty can bring it to the only fruition that is worth having. How many of us feel impelled to stop working when the person who supervises us has turned his or her back? It is a natural inclination but typical of our inborn desire to give only as much as we are compelled to for the wage we are paid. What of those of us who do just the amount of work we need do, in just the way we want to do it, and, although we are paid to give our best, we feel we do not see why we should put ourselves out to give it unless compelled to?

Many of us are inclined to forget that unless we give our best in the best possible way and spirit, we cannot expect to get the best either out of our present life or the future. Do we recognize that dishonesty is at the root of our laziness in the way we perform the work we are paid for? It is spiritually interesting to analyze our working methods and try to discover if we have ever considered Absolute Honesty in any remote way as the due, not only of those we work for, but also of work, which is, in itself, one of the greatest blessings ever bestowed upon mankind.

To us laypeople the Fellowship stresses Absolute Honesty in the practice of our spirituality as of paramount importance, not only to the religions of which we may be members, but to the living Faith of our Higher Power. How many of us are really living lives of Absolute Sincerity of spiritual purpose? Do we really practice on Monday what we have professed on Sunday? How many of us care whether the place we meet in is empty or full, as long as we are spiritually content and the meetings are not too long? Have we made much, or any, effort to get those outside to come in and to find our Program, or do we think that is the other fellow's business? Are we real members in Fellowship? Do we even know the full significance of the word *Fellowship*? Is ours a faith we are proud of when we argue about it with an outsider but one that does not make us argue within ourselves whether we are really a good example of the products of that faith? What about Absolute Honesty? If we expect others to have and practice it, we must practice it ourselves.

A B S O L U T E   P U R I T Y

Absolute Purity is not only an idea of a spiritual life demanding a clean mind in a clean body. It is a much larger word. It suggests clean conduct in business, work, and play, in our interest in world affairs, our use of our possessions, and our attitude toward relatives, friends, and acquaintances. In this sense Absolute Purity is akin to Absolute Honesty. Purity is being honest to the best possible side of our natures, mental, physical, and spiritual. It does not of necessity mean dullness. There is adventure in purity.

"Blessed are the pure in heart." The "in heart" is the secret of real purity. There is no worse hypocrite than one who is outwardly pure but unpure in heart, forgetting that although a person sees only other people, God sees the soul. All the outward restraint possible is of no significance if the heart festers with impurity. It is typical of some people who pretend to be shocked at some seeming indecency that their own secret thoughts are teeming with indecencies. They arrogate to themselves the external purity of a lovely flower inviting admiration for its exquisite quality of color and form, but behind the velvet delicacy of its petals is a heart rotten and worm eaten. When our soul stands naked before our Higher Power and God sees us in our utter simplicity, we face the only test of real purity.

Life today revolves round impurity of thought, motives, and conduct. "Keep moving at all costs!" is the cry that goes up without ceasing day and night. "Don't stand still or you'll be knocked down and trampled on! Knock the other person down before he can strike a blow at you! They intend to rob you so why not rob them first?

"Newspaper proprietors! Send up the circulation of your papers, and beat your competitors by publishing filth called 'Confessions'! Notoriety has a market value! Murderers! Sell your life story for publication to the highest bidder! There's money in it, and you may escape the gallows to enjoy it, if the lawyers haven't taken it for their fees! If you don't escape the gallows you'll have the satisfaction of knowing you'll be remembered for your crime and your confessions for many generations to come! Your name will be a household one and that's better than being a nobody! So advertise!

"You've been divorced several times? Tell the world! The general public likes that sort of thing. They'll envy you, and when you marry again they'll talk about your fascination!

You drug? Then out with your experiences! Lay bare your soul, your torments, your hideous dreams, and then your name will be bill-posted throughout the city! When you are taken before the judge, crowds will fight to get into the court. You'll be featured on the front page of the news! People will stare at you! You'll be in the limelight! Your sins are your salvation from drabness of life! So advertise them! That's Life; and Life's so short and who knows if there's anything after?"

And so the world races round. Publicity, which is mistaken for honesty; moral dirt, physical degeneracy, lying, swindling, adultery; they are not impurities, the moderns say. In this world, where everything is speed and everything is judged by its financial value, they are assets. Souls are for sale cheap. No wonder some of us ask how we can possibly live or think purely when the modern morals of the world make it impossible! Some say it is silly and a waste of time to try it. Of course it is if we do not know Peace, or want to know it, or do not realize that spiritual progress in all our affairs from the temptations that God takes away, gives back in return real happiness and constructive peace a thousandfold. The Pure in Heart do not only see God but also hear their Higher Power's will for them. They know that Absolute Purity is never in vain.

Sex is the word that either makes people pretend to shudder at its sound, or in the mind of many people sex still remains a sordid invention of Nature that is best not spoken of at any time, let alone discussed openly. To others purity is impossible. Sex is their all-in-all. Their world revolves round it and all its trappings. Sex is love to them, the vitality in an otherwise humdrum world. They earn money for it, dress for it, live for it, and dream of it. Without this blatant, absorbing sex-obsession they can conceive of no life possible for them; everything they do is traceable to sex-domination. Impurity? "What is that?" they ask. There is no such word as *impurity* to those people who have made sex their god.

Those others who deliberately put sex beyond the pale of discussion and consign it to the darkness of ignorance are often dangerous sinks of impurity themselves. Their whispers are even more destructive than the voices that shout sex from the housetops. Their veiled innuendos and allusions to sex often bring a blush to the cheek of the normal person more readily than a healthy allusion to sex, when that allusion is in its natural place. Impurity is the reason for these whisperings, not the purity those people delude themselves it is. And impurity that is disguised as purity is impurity of the most harmful kind.

In the education of the young, sex is still a bone of contention. Many elders still believe the young can be brought up as better people if they are spoon-fed fairy stories about their origin. As their children grow to adolescence, they would let their children invent ghastly mental pictures or develop a horror of sex as something unclean, rather than put sex on a normal basis for instruction when the young mind is in a receptive condition to be put wise to natural instincts and methods of propagation. Those parents and teachers who are incapable of or shudder at the thought of enlightening a young mind that needs a simple helpful explanation of sex at an opportune moment in its life, are suffering from a shame that has its roots deep in impurity. "To the pure all things are pure." The minds of the normal young receive sex instruction, helpfully given by one they respect, with the purity and reverence that is its natural right.

With certain sets of people who call themselves "intellectuals" impurity has become the fashion. A number of these "intellectuals" are really mental snobs with minds that are of little use to anyone and are filled with colossal impertinence. Writers of a certain class of fiction decry all forms of decency and purity, by their sheer audacity lulling the reading public into the belief that putting expressions and words that are not usually used in decent society into print is a sign of genius. Writers who have been given by God talents beyond the ordinary descend into depths of filth in their work that would make the average, hard-swearing but honest person disgusted. Even if literary critics condemn a porno-graphic book for its blatant indecency the sales do not suffer. Publicity of any kind is an advertisement, and an enormous number of people will rush to buy a book that has been con-demned for its indecency or, should the work be banned from public sale, offer large sums for copies that may be purchased through private channels. Beauty of word and great writing are not dead, but it will need a literary world to rid us thor-oughly of the influence of a minority of authors who would sell their souls to the Devil.

The theater and cinema are easy prey to those who would commercialize indecencies. Censors and police are vigilant in most countries to stamp out moral degeneracy in entertain-ment, but the appetite of a prurient minority demands inde-cencies, immodesty, and easy virtue in entertainment and is willing to pay well for them. So those who cater to this class of entertainment-goers use every device and subterfuge to give them what they want. Much that is not only against good taste but frankly, harmfully obscene gets past the guardians of the morals of the entertainment public. "Where there's a will there's a way" is proved constantly in the business. Films and plays are often produced publicly that make the public wonder whether any kind of censorship exists at all.

That pictorial art must shock to attract attention is the belief of some of those who have an artistic capacity. Modern art galleries and exhibitions exude suggestive nudity from their walls. Grossness is mistaken for artistry, blatancy for originality, indecency for truth, until the average person often wonders if these artists are half-wits who have never grown beyond the silly crudity of their childish sex-obsessions.

In this modern world it is believed to be impossible for anyone who lives actively to lead anything approaching a virtuous life. How can one have untainted motives in the business world, for instance, when one has to compete with the lying misrepresentations of one's competitors, who will stick at nothing to ruin one? How can one think modestly when literature, films, plays, and art rely on impurity to tickle the palate of a jaded public? How can one behave with purity when one is surrounded by people who find impurity of action the incentive to forget that we are not on earth forever and who find that "live today, for tomorrow we may be dead" is a drug that deadens them to sensitivity and remorse? What shame is there in incontinence when pseudoscientific writers tell us to allow our instincts full scope if we wish, because that is being "natural" and that being "natural" is the best way to be happy?

The only person who can answer these questions is God. Our Higher Power cannot answer them for us unless we really want to know and will listen to what God tells us. How many people believe that though the world breeds impurity God can take it away? If we believe God can meet every temptation, we must believe that God can keep us pure. God has never allowed a soul to suffer for resisting a temptation, although materially it may seem as if the results of that resistance have been a distinct loss to us. "And lead us not into temptation" means "take away from us the burden of temptation that appears too great for our human nature to resist." How many of us realize that God can enter and sanctify a mind, sweeping its darkest corners, opening spiritual windows that human means cannot move, letting in the cleansing sunlight, bathing the spiritual room that is within us all in the serenity of real purity? Feeding the mind on impurities is like feeding the body with spoiled food. Because we know the consequences to the body of such foolishness, we would not eat tainted food, why then do we feed the mind on impure food that must slowly but surely kill the soul—kill it until, because the Spirit of the Universe has been destroyed within us, we say bitterly that there is no God?

ABSOLUTE UNSELFISHNESS

Absolute Unselfishness is possible only if we have absolute love. We can be unselfish only according to the love we bear toward the object of our unselfishness. This love is not necessarily admitted to be love by the world. Sacrifice of ourselves or our interests to other people's interests, without thought of reward is, in itself, love, although we may not consciously recognize it as such when we are performing our act of unselfishness. There is more joy in Absolute Unselfishness than selfish people realize, and it is not an unfruitful joy. Absolute Unselfishness brings with it the knowledge that we are active for spiritual progress, a zeal to go on, and a certainty that, whatever we may give of ourselves—our time, money, talents, or love—it is returned by God in the very best way for us. "Cast thy bread upon the waters: for thou shalt find it after many days" is a positive fact. The bread of unselfishness that we cast upon the great ocean of human life that whirls around us does come back to us, but in the only sort of happiness that is of any use to us in this world of illusions.

Why are we envious of other people? We do not need a genius to tell us. We want things other people have that we feel we could appreciate more than they do. We are dissatisfied; life is unfair to us. Are we not all made alike? That being so, why should other people be more fortunate? We want to be brilliantly colored butterflies, not the drab moths that we think we are. As we become soured by failures and disappointments, life to us becomes one long wanting, wanting. Then sooner or later many of us say we wish we were dead, until we are awakened from our stupor of disillusion by a new and inspiring cause for another fit of fresh, revitalizing resentment against something or somebody else. How we then wallow in self-pity! No one understands us, we are misjudged people who "have never had a real chance in life." They ask, what is life to them, anyway, but hell? And so they go on Absolute

Unselfishness? What garbage! How can they be unselfish, they want to know, if they have to fight like wild beasts even to get what is due to them? Let alone have anything to be selfish about!

The curious thing is that the practice of Unselfishness takes away, as if by magic, all that self-pity, all those excuses we make to ourselves for our failures, all those feelings that we are being cheated. It definitely gives us in return the wonder of an inexplicable spiritual treasure, a description of which is impossible to put into words. It is curious because it is true, and some great truths are very curious to many of us ordinary people.

Some of us are spiritually proud with that pride that is inclined to make us thank God that we are not as other people are, and to despise those whom we feel are our inferiors in spirituality. It is that infant spiritual pride that gives us that sort of self-satisfaction that makes other people thank God they are not "religious." A virtuous feeling that comes with some self-sacrifice for the benefit of a faith we are members of or the temptation to sin which we have resisted successfully with much effort and self-restraint often tends to give us that confused attitude.

Our spiritual selves are often selfish. We have discovered a new way of spiritual living that makes us content, perhaps happier than we have ever been before. Because of this we are often apt to ignore many other people who, if we would show them how, could also find a better way of living, not by our fault-finding or superiority, but by real understanding of their difficulties and a simple demonstration of our faith and hope. We are so inclined, too, to forget that our prayers are not for ourselves alone and that they could be as beneficial to others as they can be to ourselves. Even if our efforts spiritually to help others are ineffective or if we realize that we cannot solve a problem that is beyond our human scope, we can ask for the prayers of other people to unite them to our own. That is unselfishness.

At home unselfishness is a sure foundation for harmony. It does away with friction and levels everything by love. Hatred and mistrust of one relation for another can surpass in intensity the hate and mistrusts unrelated people can have for one another. Family feuds caused by jealousy, pride, and suspicion have wrecked many lives. Who among us does not know of a family, if not our own, that is split by bitterness? It is so often an occurrence that in time, hating our relatives often becomes a sort of pastime, and we are very pleased with ourselves when we have scored some point in our favor in the game of hating those to whom we are related.

The silly spectacle of two people, closely related, ignoring each other in public because they are playing the hating game is too familiar to some of us to be funny any longer. "Give and take" is a popular remedy for unselfishness that is supposed to be able to end these feuds. But the expression would be of more practical use if the "take" were not included. "It is better to give than to receive." It is miraculous what giving with no thought of return can do to disarm the person who is opposed to us. When we give to them without a self-motive, they can honestly make no hostile retort, whether our giving be essentially material, a point of argument, or a point of personal pride. The practice of Absolute Unselfishness is a positive, workable remedy for family discord.

It is natural for growing children to question parental control, which they think is bad discipline or selfish ownership, and to make up their minds to get away from home at the first opportunity. But would not children brought up to value unselfishness understand and appreciate advice and wise control from parents who have not only instilled that unselfishness into them but also practiced it themselves?

Because it is founded on love, unlimited unselfishness between married people makes marriage proof against disagreements and divorce, and the bond between them grows stronger as the years pass. This mutual unselfishness can become, by practice, an instinct; one knows what the other needs without asking and supplies it without showing what the unselfishness costs the giver. Appreciation of the other's unselfishness does not lessen but grows as character develops. It is real partnership. Love without partnership is not marriage in the true sense of the word.

In these days pride is becoming a worldwide obsession. More than ever before people are judged and given place according to their possessions, status, feats, and accomplishments. Even some kinds of humility are the worst form of pride. Many people are proud of being "nobodies." "After all, 'I'm only a nobody'" is a silly expression of pride we hear far too often.

"For what shall a person be profited if they shall gain the whole world, and forfeit their life, or what shall a person give in exchange for their life?" Some national heroes are really world heroes. Through their sheer spirit and determination they bring new possibilities of living to everyone.

Jealousy is selfishness. That extreme demonstration of self is the most unprofitable side of humanity. It does nothing for the lasting advantage of any person and more to make the world as a whole less happy than any other failing. Jealousy is a collective wrong as well as an individual one. It can destroy a nation as easily as it can impel individuals to do things that they may regret for the rest of their lives. None of us knows to what end our jealousy about even a small and unimportant thing will lead us. A small jealousy in time can become an obsessing giant. Murder of the soul is no unusual result of a jealousy that has never been checked from its small beginnings.

To a certain degree we are all jealous and vain. Which of us can honestly say that we are not vain of our possessions, success, positions, self-restraint, liberty of action or thought, accomplishments, spiritual beliefs, agnosticism, goodness, or wickedness—or jealous of other people's? The family that eats little so that they can save enough to buy a piano they cannot play because their neighbors have a piano they can play are no more foolish than we who give up things in our lives to be equal to our neighbors in any respect.

Jealousy, envy, and pride are the cause of our own little wars that we fight with our relatives, friends, or neighbors, either in private or in public life. Before these petty resentments toward others can cease, we must make peace within ourselves. We know it is as useless to compete with someone who refuses to compete with us as it is to play a game with someone who will not play. If we stop, the war stops. If we are not interested, those who go on fighting find their joy and zest in the fight evaporating. Aloofness from wars of jealousy, envy, and pride does not necessitate our being self-satisfied; it merely requires spiritual common sense plus a sense of humor.

To these harmful few, Absolute Unselfishness seems an impossibility or a remote fantasy of a disordered mind. They think they are owners by right of possession. How often some of us say, "Possession is nine points of the law!" That is what selfishness is, when we allow our spiritual and material possessions to possess us. A person without wealth can be just as selfish as one with a fortune. We can and do waste our physical energies and spiritual possibilities as flagrantly as wealth is wasted. We waste our spiritual potentialities for individual and universal good, as much as human life and materials are wasted in abortive endeavors to make the world better by human means alone. Nothing can take away that vital invisible part of each one of us that is God's alone.

Because it is invisible, some of us think that part of us is nonexistent, forgetting that things we cannot see are often more important than things we can. By trying to the best of our abilities, under the direction of God, we can, if we will take to ourselves Absolute Unselfishness, arrest this world-spread stupendous waste of good material and equalize the positions of our fellow travelers. Neither laws nor civil bloodshed can ever accomplish this change to just administration of wealth and possessions. It is the duty of each one of us to bring spiritual common sense into the problem.

A B S O L U T E   L O V E

Absolute Love is the motive power for Absolute Honesty, Purity, and Unselfishness. We can have none of those qualities in their absolute without Absolute Love. If we have Absolute Love for God we have all those qualities for the world. We can be paragons of righteousness, but if we have not Love we are spiritually lifeless. Love generates love; and our active love today will go on spreading over life into the far future like the circles upon a lake when we throw in a stone. Love uplifts us more than any other quality; it is the color in the pattern of earthly existence.

People are gradually realizing that mind is more important than, and can be as substantial in its effects as, matter. How much more important and real in its effects than either is love! Mind in many cases is dependent on bodily condition. An enfeebled body can induce an enfeebled mind. Absolute Love is not dependent on any conditions; it needs no vast intellect or robust physical health to realize and use its unlimited powers. It is normal and practical, giving out and building up and is not an exclusive gift for the use of one type of individual more than another. It is the one indispensable part of existence that all the wealth there is, or ever has been, cannot buy. It helps those upon whom sorrow has suddenly cast a dark shadow, which seems can never be lifted, to get a right viewpoint for their future happiness. It helps the continually troubled to realize that their eyes are focused on the side of life that inevitably leads to the wasteland of utter despair, and turns their attention to the infinite possibilities of a future that has no one to say no to them but God alone.

Absolute Love transcends everything. It envelops the world, but the world will not see it. Absolute Love is the language of God and Truth in Perfection. The realization that

God loves us takes away all fears, doubts, regret, and remorse, shame of the past, dread of the future. Such love passes all understanding, bringing in its train infinite patience with others, enduring courage in life, and complete trust in God's plan for us. If we could love God with a fraction of the love God has for us, our eyes would be open to a new vision, not only for ourselves, but for all humankind.

Absolute Love is not self-negation. It is using the best of ourselves for the best of other people. In doing so, we realize that the best within us is a positive force for our own good as well as that of others. Many of us do not understand what fellowship means or that looking for self-motives in people's good actions is killing the good within ourselves. Many people look for motives in kindness that is freely given to them. "What are they hoping to get out of it?" they often think when they have been shown an unexpected generosity. Then the good offered to them loses its most potent asset, the example that God gives without thought of return or thanks.

Many people who give put too much importance on thanks, which are not so necessary to the givers of good as they suppose. "I'll never do anything for them again," a giver will say. "Why, they never even thanked me!" Should we not have others thank God for us than thank us alone? By that they are paying us the greatest tribute possible to be paid to anyone.

Absolute Love is wanted by many of us today more than anything else. If we are not to decay utterly it is our vital need. This is not pessimism. Consciousness that Absolute Love only can save us is the most optimistic piece of honesty we can face. The majority of people will not face squarely even the most pressing problems. They hope that in some way an unexpected salvation will appear from somewhere, sometime, somehow, soon, and put the world's affairs perfectly straight. In consequence, they hope they will be quite happy and comfortable again with little or no effort on their part.

But it is not quite so easy as all that to bring us at our ebb tide back to the full flood of content and prosperity. To make the scales balance again we need to face our problems honestly and to recognize what the power of God's love can do. How many people give more than a passing thought to the foolish administration of the world's, or even their country's, affairs, the ineffectiveness of Godless governments and institutions and laws for which every individual is directly responsible as a citizen? Patriotism is not enough. Fearless, boundless love of God is the only key.

Love is not only an emotion. Love is understanding. When we give understanding we give love. "A loving heart," said Thomas Carlyle, "is the beginning of all knowledge." Who welcomes this knowledge of a loving heart?

If half the problems so near to all of us could awaken even a spurt of constructive action, we should try to get down to the real solution by proving to the world that God, with God's Absolute Love for humankind, can and will, for the sake of a few, save the many who will not even know God.

Those of us who call ourselves spiritually awake must demonstrate what Absolute Love is before the world will accept it. We, whatever or whoever we may be, must accept Absolute Love as the fountain from whence the essence of our being springs. Our endeavors to make Love the very air that our souls breathe will be our best endeavors to make this world a better and happier place for all to live in. It is of no use to ourselves or to anyone to picture to ourselves Perfect Love and what it could do universally and say it is pleasant to think of but impossible to use for the good of all, so why trouble about it at all? Our concerted efforts will save us all from the unthinkable climax that unchecked class hatred may bring upon us. And unless real spiritually centered people determine now to give Love full scope in their individual life, what chance of peace is there for the whole world in the future?

Absolute Love is the Absolute Love of God. It means not only the giving of our spiritual individuality, all the human best that is in us, but also the receiving from God the peace of that quality of life God gives to the world. Love is not only doing but seeing. If we can see people in harmony and as God sees them, all things are possible for us. We must be actually and helpfully conscious of other people's existence, of their being like us, in that they are all separate individuals with urges, failings, strengths, opinions, desires, reasons, likes, and dislikes as we have. To try to ally our own individuality to theirs, so that neither we nor they will be the weaker or the stronger, but partners, mutually understanding and forgiving, living together in perfect harmony of human and spiritual brotherhood, is to understand Absolute Love.

Often, it is not so much what we give to others but what we give up for them that makes for harmony and that bond of real understanding from which love springs. God can and does give back to us so much more in return for that which we give up for our fellow travelers. No person has given up more for humanity than God could repay. Within us all we have the inexhaustible wealth of God to draw on, a wealth that is a mine within us, the treasures of which become more precious the deeper we go below the material crust of the dark earth.

YOU

*O*ur Group offers Fellowship to the world and reborn souls to society, a sane, practical Program to put right the spiritual and material problems that confront us. The Group knows no social distinctions and no spiritual laws but God's laws. It has a future for every individual, a determination to impress upon this civilization that God's plan is the only plan that is workable for the good of a world where each for all and all for each would not be a theoretical fantasy but a fact.

The Group knows that every Life that is Changed to God is definitely one more important step toward putting the world right, and that every Changed Life is one more individual set free from slavery. It has a workable message for many, for the influential, and the thinkers who work in their particular ways for the world. For those who are governed, in whatever human grade they may be, it has a practical message for their cooperation toward peace on earth and good will toward all.

Absolute Honesty? Absolute Purity? Absolute Unselfishness? Absolute Love? We must believe they are possible on earth.

We have great men and women living among us. We have the benefit of great discoveries and inventions for our better living conditions. We have great scope for the Future. God is a world necessity. We must not remain in the clouds like many people who devote their lives to studying stars they cannot touch while the real secret of the Heavens lies unheeded at their feet. God is as modern today as God was through countless yesterdays and will be in infinite tomorrows. Let us be with God, or soon we shall be nothing without God. Spiritual apathy now is not only an individual sin that will have a direct effect upon future generations, but also a sin toward God.

On the individual in everyday life rests responsibility beyond his or her understanding. On these shifting sands of life it is impossible to build a house called the Future entirely of hopes and dreams. In this swift-changing material world our possessions of today may be our debts of tomorrow. Events move swiftly now. Stability of money and morals has gone beyond the recall of conferences and laws. Hysteria and Hate are the diseases of the world. Pace has taken the place of Sanity. Our children are being born into a social madhouse.

The hour for a change approaches.

This, every individual of everyday life, is your world. This is your life to use for God and humanity or to throw away— as you choose. You select your own rules. In that you make your own laws, you are making your future resentments. In you is your fate, peace, and progress.

Do you know of even one person whose life would be happier and more fruitful if it were guided by God? You do? One—two—a dozen? Then those lives are your responsibility. We cannot all be great thinkers or talkers for God. But we can carry the message in the best way we can, with those abilities best suited for the purpose. In this life the woman whose domain is her small household is just as important to God as the Ruler of a Nation. To all of us in our different ways God gives His Challenge for a new world. It is a Challenge to You.

To you is offered Fellowship. Eager hands are held out to you. Difficulties in the way are your own making; whatever may be keeping you from the fullness of material life need not keep you from the fullness of a Surrendered life to God. Which will you have, God or Chaos?

It is *you* who hold in your hands the future spiritual and material happiness of individuals, the awakening of a sane and reconstructive policy for the united Fellowship of all peoples. It is not a dream. It is a necessity that has no alternative if Chaos is not to come. You must lead your leaders.

You means all of us.

For *you* there is work ahead; real work that has no limitations or end that anyone can foresee.

When your work here is finished, there are for you those words of the Christian writer Saint Paul: "I have fought the good fight, I have finished the course, I have kept the faith."

WHAT IS THE OXFORD GROUP?

By

THE LAYMAN WITH A NOTEBOOK

With a Foreword by

L . W . GRENSTED
Oriel Professor of the Philosophy
of the Christian Religion

TO MY FRIEND

FRANK BUCHMAN

CONTENTS

FOREWORD

The very last thing that the writer of this book would wish is that he should become widely known as a prophet of the Oxford Group Movement. Even less, if that were possible, would he claim any special authority as an exponent of its principles. For both reasons I am sure that he is right in his desire that his book should be an anonymous exposition of the principles which underlie the experience of new strength and new vision through which he has been passing. It has been written, as his friends know, with a heat of conviction which makes it rather a living document than a carefully guarded treatise. It is, for those who can understand, a piece of direct and first-hand evidence for the ways of God's working in a human life.

Yet, since anonymity carries its own risks of misunderstanding, I am glad to have the opportunity of adding this brief foreword. Characteristically individual as this book is, it yet covers so much of the ground of the experience upon which the fellowship of the Group is based, and in a form at once so systematic and so readable, that I believe that it may, under God, be used very widely to help others to understand that fellowship better, and to bring home to them that challenge of the living Christ for which and for which alone the fellowship stands.

L. W. GRENSTED
ORIEL COLLEGE,
OXFORD

THE OXFORD GROUP

'For God gave us not
a spirit of fearfulness;
but of power and love and discipline.'

2 TIMOTHY I. 7.

THE OXFORD GROUP

'And it shall be in the last days, saith God, I will pour forth
of my Spirit upon all flesh: and your sons and
your daughter shall prophesy, and your young men
shall see visions, and your old men shall dream dreams.'
—ACTS II. 17.

*Y*OU cannot belong to the Oxford Group. It has no membership list, subscriptions, badge, rules, or definite loca-
tion. It is a name for a group of people who, from every
rank, profession, and trade, in many countries, have surrendered
their lives to God and who are endeavouring to lead a spiritual
quality of life under the guidance of the Holy Spirit.

The Oxford Group is not a religion; it has no hierarchy, no
temples, no endowments; its workers have no salaries, no plans
but God's Plan; every country is their country, every man their
brother. They are Holy Crusaders in modern dress, wearing spiritual armour. Their aim is 'A New World Order for Christ, the
King'.

The Oxford Group is often confused in the minds of
strangers with the Oxford Movement. The former which, by
accident rather than by design, uses Oxford as the nominal centre
for its activities in England, is a campaign for the renaissance of
the practice among men of the truths of simple Christianity;
the latter is a Catholic renaissance within the Church of England.

The Oxford Group works within churches of all denominations, planning to bring those outside back into their folds

and to re-awaken those within to their responsibilities as Christians. It advocates nothing that is not the fundamental basis of all Christian Faith, and takes no side in sectarian disputes. It seeks to enable us to use our beliefs to their best advantage for ourselves and for the world in general. This means living as near as we can, by God's help, to the life He has mapped out for us. When we diverge from His plan for us we can, by surrendering our lives to Him, get back to that plan again, and by our Christian endeavours to live as parallel as we can to Christ's life here on earth and, with God's Guidance to show us how we can best do that, we can continue on that plan and bring it to fruition.

Those of us who have seen the wonders of the results of the life changing of the Oxford Group can only describe them as modern miracles. Men and women, who have never before realized that Sin can kill not only the soul but mind, talents, and happiness as surely as a malignant physical disease can kill the body, have found that surrender to God, in actuality as well as in theory, means a new lease of life which brings with it a fuller joy of living than they have realized was possible for them. They have been reborn to the world as well as reborn to God. All their appreciations of the best and worth-while things in life, their work, their capacity for human intercourse, have become really alive; living has now limitless depth and breadth and height and is no longer a stifling prison of Sin. Christ has ceased to be a figure in Religion to them and becomes a Reality with boundless modern wisdom, an understanding and really helpful Presence who is very near to them in all they think, do, and say. They know now the secret of real happiness on earth; the spiritual profit given by the right kind of outlook; a real sense of the values of life, and a true sense of spiritual and material proportion. In fact, they have become sane.

Undeniable evidence of the fruits of the work of the Oxford Group has been published too recently to need repetition here. Books detailing but a few of the marvels that have resulted from its changing of lives can be obtained easily. Spoken evidence from lay and clerical witnesses can be heard at Group meetings or at larger gatherings, which are arranged from time to time in various countries, called by the Group, House-parties. Thousands of these witnesses are convicted by the evidence in their own lives of what the life changing of the Oxford Group has done for them and can do for all. Witnesses will go anywhere at any time to help any one whose life has become a burden of Sin, and will stand by until that person has been set free from trouble and brought to a true understanding of Christ and life. No soul has sunk too far, no case for spiritual cure can go beyond their scope. The knowledge that we are in need and have a need for change in our lives is all that is necessary for these life changers to work on. They know for sure that the age of Christ's miracles has not passed from us, and for these miracles they are willing instruments for a willing God.

Families have been united, marriages saved from divorce, husbands and wives brought together with a new understanding love between them, lonely people made to see that there are many who are eager for and will be honoured by their friendship; sinners who are obsessed by their sins find that they can be set free and reborn into spiritual liberty; would-be suicides live to be useful and happy men and women; the young find that there is a purpose in their future which is not dull and uninteresting but adventurous and worth growing towards; and the old learn that each day more of life given to them is a day they can live to its full, and that all vain regrets for their pasts are as useless as a storm that has passed over and is gone.

The aims of the Oxford Group are to bring into the world the realization of the power of the Holy Spirit as a force for spiritual and material stability and betterment of the world; to awaken in us as individuals the knowledge that we are dissipating our spiritual inheritance and that Sin is the frustration of God's Plan for us all. It sets out to make the world understand that spiritual common sense is of more practical value and use to mankind than selfish piety or blind paganism.

The working beliefs of the Group are not misty ideals; they are practical standards within the scope of any one who will give his or her life, powerful, insignificant, interesting, or prosaic as it may be, in the world, into God's absolute keeping. There is no reason why this giving of our lives to God should mean our being pious or religious bores. Neither should it mean that we have to give up our ordinary obligations or duties. It means we surrender to God everything that stands between Him and us.

The Oxford Group has four points which are the keys to the kind of spiritual life God wishes us to lead. These points are:

1. Absolute Honesty.

2. Absolute Purity.

3. Absolute Unselfishness.

4. Absolute Love.

The average unchanged person on seeing these points or hearing of them asks: 'But how can I—or any one—be *absolutely* honest or pure or unselfish or loving in a world like this?'

Jesus Christ kept to these four points in their fullness. He was a man without home, possessions, or earthly commitments. The nearer we live to the Absolute in these four points the nearer we are to Christ, whether it means being without a home, possessions, or earthly responsibilities; or our taking on more responsibilities. God knows the zest we put into our fight for a life founded on Christ principles. He knows the difficulties of circumstances, and the influence of environment that confront the real Christian at every step, and because He can gauge the sincerity of our vision He does not too harshly condemn our stumbles. We have not the knowledge which would enable us to judge if any man or woman has been able to live a life absolutely as Christ would have him or her live it; but the Oxford Group do know that placing these necessary four points for a Christian life as absolute ones is placing Christ as the absolute example to which, by the help of God, we can aspire.

The Oxford Group four points are the basis of beauty of thought, word, and deed. They may not be so unattainable as we may suppose, but very few can or have ever lived lives of Absolute Honesty, Purity, Unselfishness, and Love. 'For all have sinned and come short of the glory of God', St. Paul tells us. It is doubtful if even a mystic, giving up his life to pious contemplation, lives a life founded on these four points in their fullness. It is a matter of argument whether his shutting himself away from human contact is Absolute Love for his fellow men; it certainly seems to the uninitiated to be selflessness in a negative form. The saints of this world, past and present, are those who whilst still leading a helpful material life for other people fight relentless warfare against their own temptations and the dire results of Sin in other people. They are the Saint Georges who persistently strive to kill the dragon of Sin which will not lie down and die gracefully. Daily they are singed by the fiery breath from the dragon's devouring jaws, crushed to earth by his huge unwieldy body; but they rise again, pick up the sword of a Christian life dropped when they fell into Sin and, by God's grace, forgiven their fall, they commence once again their fight for Absolute Honesty, Purity, Unselfishness, and Love.

To be spiritually reborn, and to live in the state in which these four points are the guides to our life in God, the Oxford Group advocate four practical spiritual activities:

1. The Sharing of our sins and temptations with another Christian life given to God, and to use Sharing as Witness to help others, still unchanged, to recognize and acknowledge their sins.

2. Surrender of our life, past, present, and future, into God's keeping and direction.

3. Restitution to all whom we have wronged directly or indirectly.

4. Listening to, accepting, relying on God's Guidance and carrying it out in everything we do or say, great or small.

These spiritual activities have proved indispensable to countless numbers who are living Changed lives. They are not new ideas nor inventions of the Oxford Group. They are the simple tenets of simple Christianity.

The Oxford Group is not one group. It is a collection of groups active for Christ in many countries, meeting in ordinary places where ordinary men and women are accustomed to meet in the course of their daily lives. They are similar to the groups of early Christians who met in places hidden from their oppressors, to keep alight the torch of Christianity. The Oxford Groups do not find it necessary to hide—at the moment—but their mission is the same as that of the early Christians—the redemption of individuals and nations from Sin, and to keep alive the Faith for which Christ came on earth, suffered and died, so that every man, woman, and child in this world might see and understand that Perfection of Life to which all of us would attain if we, too, would be Christ-like.

Oxford Group meetings are held anywhere, in large towns as in small villages. Witnesses for what Christ means in lives Changed to God awaken others to the possibilities of what this new quality of life may have in store for them. Plans are formed, by the help of God, to bring those who are spiritually asleep or in spiritual need into the fellowship; and the best ways to carry these out are discussed. Action for Christ to these Groups is joy; the utter belief and full realization of man's present pressing need for Christ-control is their incentive. The Groups may be large or small, but however small they may be they are vital beacons of a living Christianity in a fast darkening world.

To those who are strangers to the Group in action a House-party is the simplest and most informative means for seeing the effects and getting to the best understanding of the Group's work. These House-parties are held at certain intervals in various countries. House-parties is an apt name for these cosmopolitan gatherings, for they are not in the nature of religious conventions, nor are they revivalist meetings. Guests at these House-parties are treated as guests; they meet on an equal social footing, what-ever may be their social status elsewhere; gloom is conspicuous by its absence, and there is more laughter at an Oxford Group House-party than at many ordinary social gatherings.

At these House-parties Christ and His Power, His Life and His Plans are discussed with such a freedom from empty piety that the stranger, unaware perhaps of the direct methods of the Oxford Group, is often staggered and perplexed before he is enthralled by the desire to probe deeper into the healthy aspect of this Christianity of the Oxford Group. Individual spiritual needs are attended to in a sensible and business-like way. The affairs and problems of the world are discussed directly and con-structively without partisanship. All are allowed to contribute their views, for before all is the possibility that God will ordain that one of those present may at some time be an ace for Christ in the game of world reconstruction.

The Bible is studied at House-parties for its modern bearing on our individual and collective needs. Mixed meetings are held for Witness and Discussion. There are special meetings where women are in close counsel with women, men with men, clergy with clergy, members of a particular profession with other members of that profession, people of one locality with others of the same, inhabitants of a country with their compatriots. Attendance at any service which may be arranged at a local place of worship is not compulsory for guests; members of a faith attend the services of that faith as that faith demands or as their religious convictions dictate.

The social aspect of these House-parties is not forgotten; all are free to do as they wish; come as they please and go when they want. To the stranger an Oxford Group House-party, cosmopolitan in nature, with social equality, and perfect fellowship, is a glimpse of what the foundation of a new Christian civilization might be.

Laymen of many nationalities, creeds, professions, and outlook form the nucleus of these gatherings, and it is not unusual for a thousand clergy of various denominations and a score of bishops to travel long distances to attend them, not only to discover there the real spiritual needs of modern people but the spiritual needs within themselves. But the House-parties are neither dominated nor restricted by the presence of the clergy. They are for men and women with a definite purpose—Changing lives to Change the world to Christ.

Tremendous interest was taken in the recent visits of the travelling teams to America, Canada, and South Africa by the peoples of these countries. Thousands in all grades of society flocked to main and overflow meetings, eager to listen to these modern crusaders for Christ. The simple directness of the delivery of the teams' testimonies and their obvious sincerity when they spoke of what Changed lives meant to them Changed many others to real Christianity. In Canada Mr. Bennett, the Prime Minister, said to the Oxford Group:—'As Wesley saved England from the effects of the French revolution, so the forces which you so powerfully represent are the only ones that can save civilization to-day.'

In South Africa the visit of a team of the Group resulted in the bringing about of better racial understanding and reforms which will have a lasting effect on the life of that Dominion. A well-known South African statesman has said that if the work of the Group continues to grow in South Africa during the next few years as it has in the past, there will soon be no racial problems there.

'As cold water is to a thirsty soul so is good news from a far country', and other nations have given as enthusiastic a welcome to the teams who have left behind them active local groups to carry on their work and to multiply daily in numbers and in spiritual strength. The Oxford Group is now a far-flung battle-line for Christianity. If the forces it represents are to save Civilization, every thinking Christian will at once realize that in the inevitable clash with the anti-Christs, which approaches nearer as the world spins towards the end of the present social era, there must be no gaps in that battle-line.

The story of the origin of the Oxford Group is too well known to make it necessary to repeat it fully here. Dr. Frank Buchman, a Lutheran minister, came to England from America a dissatisfied man, feeling that his work for the spiritual and social welfare of young men there had been seriously hampered by a difference of opinion with a governing committee. Whilst in England he caught a vision of a Christ-led world untrammelled by Sin. Other people have caught that selfsame vision, and Frank Buchman claims no special distinction for the vision coming to him. But, unlike some of the other people, he went right ahead to make that vision a practical reality. It meant the cutting of all personal ties, the sublimation of his personal ambitions, and making the wide world the only place he could call home. He travelled for years, Changing a few lives here and there. Eventually, at the request of two Anglican bishops in the Far East, he came to Cambridge, where he Changed two undergraduates. With these he paid a visit to Oxford. It is quite permissible for Cambridge to compete with Oxford in sports, but for Cambridge to send two undergraduates to Oxford to Change the University to God was, to say the least, novel. But from this visit to Oxford where these two undergraduates witnessed for Christ there sprang up those modern pilgrimages, in the form of House-parties at Oxford, which are now attended by thousands of people from all over the world. This fact, added to the appending of the word Oxford by the South Africans to a team from the Group which visited that Dominion a few years ago, has settled the name Oxford Group on Frank Buchman's endeavour to realize the vision he once caught.

Frank Buchman's strength lies in his optimism for Christ; Christ not as a far-away Person but as the Spirit of Love for all men, walking this earth with us, facing up to our troubles with us, happy when we are happy, consoling with a balanced and practical consolation when we are in need of consolation; correcting us with a correction that does not make us feel inferior or hopeless because of our mistakes and failings but stronger for experience and better able to get a normal focus on our weaknesses. Christ, to Frank Buchman, is not a prop for our human frailties, not a nurse behind whom we should hide in moments of moral cowardice, but a friend who is united to each of us individually in an understanding and progressive sympathy.

Frank Buchman is not an ascetic. He wears no distinctive garb, affects no unusual manner, and makes no claim to an unusual personality. The extent of his tireless devotion to work for Christ will never be fully reckoned by any man; his unfailing optimism and belief in the infinite spiritual possibilities of humanity and his willingness to place himself at all times of the night and day at the disposal of those in spiritual need are part of the Oxford Group's Fellowship in Christ, and require no testimonial here. He is a spiritual dynamo with very human common sense; and yet when others are carrying out with effectiveness and sincerity the work in which he believes with every fibre of his being he is content to be no more than a fervent 'Amen'.

The Oxford Group do not set up to be a collection of paragons of the Virtues nor are they a set of religious bores. They are the normal men and women we would meet on any normal occasion and who would no more ram religion down our throats than we would ram it down theirs. They might, as calmly as we might ask them to pass the salt, tell us that God has guided them to speak to us because, by that means, they have become aware that we are in spiritual trouble and need help; but if, in reply, we looked at them as if we suspected they were mad it would neither shake their poise nor damp their cheerful ardour.

Because they themselves are not saints but sinners who know God, they have made the word sinner a common bond for humanity.

Undue emotionalism, religious hysteria, and neurosis are banned entirely by the Oxford Group. They have no use for them whatever. The business of the Group is to eradicate them from the spiritual system and so set life free for Absolute Honesty of living. They know by experience that Absolute Love can conquer all evil; that Absolute Truth is as personally necessary for those who preach it as it is for those it is preached at; that too much dependency on other people for our happiness is weakness, and that fellowship with Christ is strength.

The Oxford Group will be reviled and persecuted; material anti-Christs and intellectual Pharisees will mock it, but because it is founded on the intrinsic simple Christian truths and is walking bravely towards the light, it must survive and grow stronger. That it will be persecuted is only to be expected. *Which of the prophets did not your fathers persecute?*

S I N

'*Be subject therefore unto God;*
but resist the devil, and he will flee from you.
Draw nigh to God, and He will draw nigh to you.
Cleanse your hands, ye sinners;
and purify your hearts, ye doubleminded.'
JAMES IV. 7 AND 8.

'*Behaviour is a mirror*
in which everyone displays his image.'
GOETHE.

S I N

*'For all have sinned,
and fall short of the glory of God.'*
ROMANS III. 23.

'SIN', the Oxford Group puts it bluntly, 'is anything that keeps us from God or from one another.'

Sin is a word many people fight shy of; to them the very word is out of date; it smacks of street-corner salvation meetings; they think only people who are behind the times believe in Sin these days. In their conversations it is seldom used, except, perhaps, to raise a laugh. But what colourful pictures Sin conjures up! Sin! When fashionable preachers call it scarlet and denounce the fashionable sins of their fashionable congregations in their fashionable churches there is a thrill in Sin for some. They delight in going to hear their sins denounced; it is an entertainment well worth paying for! It gives them a feeling that to be denounced as wicked is a sign of social success. How very often are 'The Sins of Mayfair' or 'The Sins of Hollywood', the subjects of articles in the Sunday press, read with envious appreciation by those above stairs as well as those below!

Pathological psychology has become a fashionable cult of recent years. The subconscious has been enthroned, like a mental giant which is supposed to rule our destinies and be at the root of all we think, do, or say. Any failing or abnormality, however hideous, can be blamed on our subconscious mind, which has become a gold-mine for those who seek to profit by the frailties of human nature.

Sin and temptation to Sin are called by the modern intelli-
gentsia any name but their own. To these 'high-brows' sins are
repressed desires; inhibitions; fixations; morbid introspection;
suppression of natural instincts and other words ending in 'ism',
'phobia', 'mania'—anything but what they are—just plain Sin.
When we ask one of these intelligent people, 'Are you ever
tempted to sin?' and they reply, 'Certainly not! But I have a suppressed desire to shoplift', it is about as logical as an exercise in
a French primer which says, 'Have you seen the pen of my aunt?'
and replies, 'No, but my grandmother keeps bees.'

Sin is a disease with consequences we cannot foretell or
judge; it is as contagious as any contagious disease our bodies may
suffer from. The sin we commit within this hour may have
unforeseen dire consequences even after we have long ceased to
draw living breath. That is not a morbid surmise; it is a truth.
None of us knows the future; few of us know the consequences
of even our simplest normal actions; so how can we know where
the direct or indirect effects of our sins end?

Like physical disease Sin needs antiseptics to prevent it from
spreading; the soul needs cleaning as much as the body needs it.
When what we call conscience pains us with remorse, it is the
spiritual equivalent to the pains our body sends us as signals
that it is disordered and needs attention.

Sin is a definite disorder of the soul. George Eliot has said:

> 'There is no sort of wrong deed of which a man can bear
> the punishment alone; you can't isolate yourself, and say that
> the evil which is in you shall not spread. Men's lives are as
> thoroughly blended with each other as the air they breathe;
> evil spreads as necessarily as disease. Every sin causes suffering
> to others beside those who commit it.'

Unhappiness to us and others, discontent, and, frequently,
mental and bodily ill health are the direct results of Sin. It needs
no religious science, deep study of the power of thought, nor
psycho-analysis to make us realize that. Morbidity of mind must

affect the physical health. If we can be absolutely truthful to ourselves we can analyse our sins for ourselves and trace their mental and physical effects. Sins can dominate us mentally and physically until we are their abject slaves. We cannot get rid of them by deciding to think no more about them; they never leave us of their own accord, and unless they are cut out by a decided surgical spiritual operation which will destroy them, roots and all, and set us free from their killing obsession, they grow in time like a deadly moss within us until we become warped in outlook not only towards others but towards ourselves.

Some people think they are not sinners. If we were to ask them what their sins are they would be unable to tell us because they would say they are not aware they have any, nor could they, cudgel their brains though they might, quite understand what Sin means to them. These are the 'nice' type of sinners who say they are not troubled by Sin. But if we were to ask them a few direct questions about their motives, outlook, or views on other people, if they are absolutely honest, they would see by what they think and say that Sin is a kind of pastime to them which they call being 'natural' or 'outspoken'. The sins of 'nice' people are often sins 'nasty' people would despise themselves for, if they had them. We all know 'nice' sinless sinners who need that surgical spiritual operation as keenly as the most miserable sinner of us all.

The Oxford Group believes, and rightly, that once we have shared our sins with another Christian and surrendered them to God our sins are best forgotten. But some people cannot forget their sins even after they believe they have begun a new spiritual life. Listen to those who are Sin-conscious and cannot really relinquish their sins to God, and so get rid of them once and for all. How they delight in retelling their sins from which they have been 'converted', but, although they refrain from admitting it, without at the same time gaining spiritual regeneration. How they cling to the glamour of their sins of the past as if fascinated by them! They are not new men but merely men with a past.

Pride in Sin, whether we say we are regenerated from it or

whether we publish it to the world under the cloak of shame, is a decided weakness some of us suffer from. Our souls must be either clean or dirty; they cannot be both at the same time. Those of us who cannot get away from our past wrong-doing, in spite of thinking we are spiritually regenerated, have missed the point of Divine forgiveness, which is, in reality, plain cancellation.

True happiness is a life without Sin; a life founded on trust in God; the life of a disciple of Christ. It is the happiness that compels others to seek it because they see that surrender of Sin casts out fear of man, as of the past and the future.

No one makes sin but ourselves. Temptation is not action. It is an invitation we can accept or refuse. This invitation is often so worded or pictured in our minds that refusal seems beyond the power of our refusing. Because they are so often the most enjoyable part of sinning, in the same way that anticipation of a pleasurable event in life is often so much more enjoyable than the actual event itself, temptations are the allure of Sin. If, as they come to us, we can give these invitations of Sin to God for His answer, we have the certain knowledge that they will not be too strong for us to resist. Under the all-powerful light of Christ they shrink back into the darkness from whence they came.

In the 'I' in the word Sin, the Oxford Group tells us, lies the secret of Sin's power. The 'I', or the ego, is more important to sinners than spiritual health; all we do contrary to Christ's teaching is traceable to it. If we can surrender that 'I' to God Sin goes with it; when we live without that 'I' in our lives we are without Sin. 'I' is a little letter with big responsibilities. It is the one letter in the alphabet that has a personality.

Every time we try to move forward spiritually that 'I' confronts us. It is the fence we put up to mark our very own part of existence from that of other people's when we want to think we are different from everybody else. 'I'm sure you can't understand that I am not the same as other people', we say. '*I* am so very different. *I* have a good excuse for doing what *I* did. *I* know it's no use *my* explaining to you. But I know what *I* am. *I* ... *I* ... *I* ...', and so the 'I' in that little word Sin dominates us, making us feel that our 'I' is tremendously important in the scheme of things; whilst all the time it means that we are looking only at ourselves and are completely oblivious of God.

Individual self-interest is the causation of world sin. The Oxford Group vision of a world set free from the destroying influence of that Sin is not vague idealism; it is a definitely possible spiritual realization that can be brought about by an army of Life Changers.

SHARING
FOR CONFESSION
AND WITNESS

*'Having therefore obtained the help that is from God,
I stand unto this day testifying both to small and great.'*
ACTS XXVI. 22.

*'At the mouth of two witnesses or three
shall every word be established.'*
—2 CORINTHIANS XIII. 1.

SHARING

*'Many also of them that had believed came,
confessing, and declaring their deeds.'*
—ACTS XIX. 18.

SHARING of sins as practised by the Oxford Group is sharing in the ordinary sense of the word; in plain language it is telling, or talking over, our sins with another whose life has already been surrendered to God or, if we have already surrendered, assisting others to surrender by openly—as we are guided—laying our past sins or present temptations alongside theirs, so that they may be able better to recognize and bring to light those sins which have stood between them and God.

Sharing on this basis is, in practice as well as in theory, not only good comradeship but very sound psychologically. 'Two minds are better than one' is an old saying which is more true when the subject in discussion is common to both parties, and Sin is certainly common to everybody. Sharing—call it 'mutual confession' if you wish—is not a new idea recently devised by an emotional mind but one of the rudiments of simple Christianity long since gone out of practice, except in certain faiths that have retained Confession to God via a priest. The sacrament of Penance for many people is a useful and excellent disciplinary religious act.

'Get it off your chest and you'll feel better' is wise advice from a wise friend to those of us who are troubled by life and feel that if we are Sin-obsessed any longer we shall lose our faith in humanity as well as in ourselves. Mental healers, whether they be secular or religious, recognize the value of our 'getting it off our chests'. Their treatment cannot be efficacious nor their understanding of our symptoms complete if we cannot do that thoroughly. Of recent years mental doctoring of all kinds and guises has become popular, often reviving as new scientific discoveries old truths based on a simple understanding of human nature. These metaphysical or psychopathologic doctors or healers have taken these old truths and adapted them to modern requirements, sometimes with excellent results, sometimes destroying where they have no power to rebuild. Simple sins are often treated by these mental practitioners as inhibitions, and human temptations as mental disorders, and it is not surprising that when these have been removed they immediately open doors to others, sometimes of a worse type.

As Jesus Christ says: 'When the unclean Spirit is gone out of a man, he walketh through dry places, seeking rest and finding none. Then he saith, I will return to my house from whence I came out; and when he is come, he findeth it empty, swept and garnished. Then goeth he, and taketh unto himself seven other spirits more wicked than himself, and they enter in and dwell there: and the last state of that man is worse than the first.'

A medical practitioner can only do us real good when we are physically ill if he finds out by asking us, or by his own deductions, the nature of our illness and then endeavours to put health in the place of our sickness—sins are symptoms of spiritual sickness. Telling our sins to a practicing Christian, as we would tell our physical symptoms to a medical practitioner, enables us not only to find the cure for our spiritual sickness but find out how to take on a new lease of spiritual health.

No one will ever realize to what extent the Holy Spirit can work through the spiritual to alleviate the troubles of the mental and physical. It is only known that the Holy Spirit can give limitless power of resistance to any disease which is caused by morbidity of outlook and the feeling that the physical is predominant in life. Setting the mind free through truth can work mental and physical wonders.

Sins are weeds that flourish and choke. If we alone cannot pull them out of our own gardens we must have some one to do the weeding for us, to help us burn them on the rubbish-heap and then, after we have set fire to them, we can turn our backs on them and walk away towards a new life. Sharing our sins brings them into the open light, giving them their proper spiritual status, grading them according to their importance to us, making us acknowledge their existence; they are no longer bogies but hard facts to be faced squarely and in due time eradicated by God's help. No man is sinless; that is the common ground for Sharing.

'Confess therefore your sins one to another, and pray one for another, that ye may be healed.' To some of us that sounds very easy on paper but very difficult or almost impossible in actual practice. 'How could I confess *everything*—all my sins even to some one who knows me very well? I have sins my closest friends do not suspect my having. Why, I couldn't even put them into words!' How many of us ordinary people think like that! We maintain a strange delusion that we are very exclusive people and that our sins are so very original; we really believe that if we did confess the Christian to whom we confessed would open his or her eyes very wide and look at us as if we had taken leave of our senses. But if we talk over our sins with any one whose life is God-directed our sins are not very flattering to our belief in their originality, because the surprising and healthy discovery the stranger makes in Sharing is that all his sins are also the sins of others. This discovery lifts from us the feeling of isolation and despair of Self. We find we can give our sins into another's keeping with as much relief as we would discard a heavy great-coat on a hot summer's day, and the cooling zephyrs of God-given reason go through our unrestricted soul and body, and we rejoice in new-found freedom and exultant hope in the future.

The discovery that our sins are often the sins of our neighbour gives a particularly healthy outlook to the young. Suicides by young people attributable to temporary insanity are often caused by the feeling that there is no escape from sins they believe peculiar to themselves. The agony of the young mind, obsessed and warped by natural sins of the body that could easily be placed on a normal basis for eradication by an understanding talk with one who has been through that agony and emerged, by Christ's help, a free human being, is indescribable. Youthful sins in time often become harmful fixed habits with a resulting bad inferiority complex. The average adolescent mind is a delicate structure, impressionable, eager for adventure, timorous of criticism, reaching out towards the glamorous climax of full experience, to enjoy the fruition of the urgent desires that must surge up as the body develops.

A father who Shares with his son the knowledge that he, too, went through the phase that his son now finds so torturous to his physical and spiritual outlook: an elder brother Sharing with a younger, a friend with a friend, can lay simply and easily those ghosts which the psycho-analyst can only eradicate by prolonged effort—if he eradicate them at all.

'And pray one for another', advised St. James. What sound advice we can find that injunction in all our difficulties! In Sharing it is no less of real aid than at any other time, for then it is taking another's burden, putting it into words and placing it before God. The consciousness that there is another human being who will pray to God that our sins will be taken from us and ask this of Him with as much urgency and sincerity as if those sins were his own is one of the most beautiful and real qualities of Christian fellowship. To those of us who have never had this experience a new and unforgettable spiritual discovery is in store.

St. James, realizing the use of the Sharing of sins, tells us that it is necessary 'that ye may be healed'. In fact it is an essential preliminary act before Surrendering our lives to God so that our spiritual selves are healed of the sickness of Sin.

To those of us—and there are many—who need God-guided counsel the fellowship of other men and women who know how difficult it is for us really to believe our sins are forgiven us, and who know that putting our sins and spiritual problems into words to another makes us absolutely honest with God, Sharing is not only a necessity but a distinct blessing. Sharing does not mean that we have to go up or down to another person's level. It is not patronage or superiority on either side. It is two people having a common interest—Sin—and getting a healthy viewpoint on it.

'Why shouldn't I go straight to God if I want to confess my sins? Why should I bother about another person interfering? The right and only person for my confession is God.' Some people, when Sharing is explained to them, say this, and often with indignation. It is a natural point of view to many, but it would be perhaps unchristian of us to ask them if they do confess to God and how much they confess and how much they keep back. We can, however, tell them that we do not deny that they can go straight to God if they wish and God will forgive them, but that if they wish for a sure and certain knowledge that their past sins—and all of them—are to be wiped out, once and for all, these sins must be brought into the open and honestly faced. To put them into words, before Christ with another Christian, as a witness, is the only healthy way of making sure that the spiritual system is virtually cleansed.

It would be idle of us to pretend that everybody needs to Share in order to live a real Christian life. None of us can judge how another man or woman stands with God, but no real Christian person could refute Sharing on the plea of confessing direct to God, because that person would realize that by talking over with a sin-burdened soul their own difficulties and compensations of living in Christ, he or she would be able to bring that soul into communion with God.

Sharing in no way trespasses on or takes the place of Confession before a priest, should this Confession be part of any of our faiths. The Oxford Group, working within the Churches, does not in any way claim that Sharing in the sense of confession is their spiritual prerogative or their religious invention. They definitely recognize that Sharing is an invaluable aid to reclaiming lives for God and that the nominal faith of the person is not of so much importance as the fact that that person, after being Changed, can return to his or her faith and become a spiritually alive member of it and be able to use its sacraments with a new understanding and renewed spiritual vitality. There is no Christian Church with none of its flock outside its sacraments, nor is there any Church with the Christ Spirit which would not welcome back a stray sheep, however dubious 'orthodoxy' might think the means used by the shepherd to bring it back to the fold again.

Sharing does not mean divulging indiscretions which involve other people by name. It means confessing our part in our sinning. Placing the blame on others and making excuses for our weaknesses is not Sharing; it is merely negative selfish talk. On the other hand, some of us find it hard not to let exhibitionism in a mild form enter everything we do concerning ourselves. We always want to be thought clever and important even when we talk about our sins. We can hardly resist painting our sins in bright colours and making ourselves heroes and heroines of the great spiritual conflicts we have fought, although we may have succumbed to Sin in the fight. Pride is as subtle as the Serpent; it can enter even our accusations against ourselves, giving us, although we may not acknowledge it, a piquant enjoyment of our confessions.

Confessions shared become the property of God, not man. Every live Christian recognizes this, and should have no fear that such frankness will become the property of other men. Our private lives remain our private lives. The past is with God; we have only the future before us.

Instinctive knowledge of human nature will prevent our having qualms about the Christian person we Share with. All of us meet on occasions those who are complements to our own natures; those we feel instinctively will 'understand' or have passed through the very phase of Sin that we are passing through and with whom we know our confessions will remain sacred from other men. Those are the Christian people in whom we should confide our spiritual difficulties.

Sharing is not a question of sympathy; the less sympathy, as mere sympathy, there is in it, and the more common sense spiritual assistance and God-given understanding the better for us.

Some of us wallow in our remorse; it is only with great difficulty that we can refrain, if we refrain at all, from Sharing our sins with any one, anywhere, at any time. This is the old foolish self which will not lie down and succumb in proper decency. It is a form of self-advertisement which no life that has, in truth, been changed to God knows in the least degree. It is therefore essential that we should make perfectly certain that our confessions once shared and forgiven are forgotten, except when we bring them out as dead specimens in witness of the living work the love of Christ has done for us.

There are in all our lives people we know and meet who would be happier and more free if they were not weighed down with Sin. They are the charge of all active Christians. They are the God-given opportunity for us to be able to make them say with the author of Hebrews: 'Therefore let us also, seeing we are all compassed about with so great a cloud of witnesses, lay aside every weight, and the sin which doth so easily beset us, and let us run with patience the race that is set before us.'

WITNESS

'We are ambassadors therefore on behalf of Christ,
as though God were intreating by us:
we beseech you on behalf of Christ,
be ye reconciled to God.'

—2 CORINTHIANS V. 20.

*T*HE Oxford Group is Witness for Christ—an Ambassador conveying His goodwill to men in a world in which goodwill among nations is conspicuous by its absence. Its assets are a conviction of the existence of a living Christ and proof of God's forgiveness and the power of the Holy Spirit. These are not assets that make an ambassador rich in worldly goods or assured of a life of comfort, nor are they a sure passport to the whole world. People are as incredulous of the existence and power of Christ now as they were when they actually saw Him in the flesh and would not believe He was the Son of God.

But the Oxford Group goes on with its work; fearless Witnesses for Christ the world over bring others to Him by Absolute Honesty and conviction of what He, since they surrendered to a life of spiritual truth, has done for them.

Witness is Sharing with others the main reasons and the concrete results of our surrender to God. Just talking Christianity and all it should mean to others is of little use when the world talks too much already. 'Faith apart from works', said St. James, 'is barren.' The Oxford Group's joy in living and working in itself manifests Christ better than any words could do. It uses the power of Christ to Change other people's lives. Guidance of God shows the best way of approach, what is best for witnesses to testify from their own lives, and when and how to bring the unchanged to God. They must not forget for a moment that they are human, and have temptations as strong as other men's and that, but for the grace of God, they would be unhappy in their souls. Their simplicity and directness do more to change their testimony with conviction than the finest rhetoric or specious arguments.

'And we are witnesses of these things; and so is the Holy Ghost, whom God hath given to them that obey Him', we read in the Acts of the Apostles. Personal proof of experience can do more than the best of theories. These Oxford Group witnesses have felt

Christ working in their own lives and the Spirit of Christ has walked beside them. They tell of what they themselves know as a positive truth. Generalization and guess-work are not in their programme. It is not surprising, therefore, that they are rapidly rekindling the fire of living Christianity and that the quickening glow from it is making people, even in far-off lands, wonder at this revitalizing challenge which is being issued to the world.

People in need are more inclined to tell us the truth about themselves if they know we are telling them the truth about ourselves. This is the foundation of the mutual trust which is essential when we witness in order to bring others to a Life Change. In families this mutual trust is invaluable in that it enables barriers of age and divers temperaments to be broken down and each can testify for Christ. Members of families whose tastes differ often find the serious mention of Christianity by one of their number rather an awkward topic. Witnessing to our relations is often more difficult than witnessing to friends or acquaintances. In modern homes they would say that 'it is hardly the thing to do' because it embarrasses them. But, given trust in the witness's sincerity, and the definite proof of Christ's influence in the witness's life, the possibilities of one member changing the whole are infinite. This the Oxford Group has proved.

We can all be witnesses for Christ, all of us who are aware of what the power of Christ has done for us. If we can say with St. John:—*'And the life was manifested, and we have seen and bear witness and declare unto you the life, the eternal life, which was with the Father, and was manifested unto us'*, we have a message to give the world. This message must be one not only of hope but of concrete proof of the Christ who was manifested unto us. It means telling others of our own experiences in Sin, of our Surrender, and after; of the power of God guidance in our lives and the spiritual strength given us to overcome our present difficulties, in accordance with the needs of those to whom we witness. We have to remember that it is our convictions that will convince other people; that half measures will be as fruitless as no measures at all. Our honesty will invite honesty from others. Nothing else will.

Those of us who realize what Sharing meant to us when we were tired of ourselves, tired of the world's problems against which we felt impotent, tired of sinning and tired of living, know that in Sharing we understand what George Meredith meant when he wrote:

'We drank the pure daylight of honest speech.'

S U R R E N D E R

'Know ye not that ye are a temple of God,
and that the Spirit of God dwelleth in you?'
1 CORINTHIANS III. 16.

The longing for ignoble things;
The strife for triumph more than truth;
The hardening of the heart, that brings
Irreverence for the dreams of youth;
All thoughts of ill, all evil deeds,
That have their roots in thoughts of ill:
Whatever hinders or impedes
The action of the nobler will;
All these must first be trampled down
Beneath our feet, if we would gain
In the bright fields of fair renown
The right of eminent domain.

H. W. LONGFELLOW.

SURRENDER

'God is a Spirit:
and they that worship him
must worship in spirit and truth.'
—ST. JOHN IV. 24.

URRENDER to God is our actual passing from a life of Sin to a life God-Guided and Christ-Conscious; in other words it is the giving up of our old ineffective spiritual lives and taking on life of spiritual activity in everything we think, do, or say. By making complete restitution for wrongs done to others, to ensure that all debts are paid, and by ending all wrong associations, a Changed life renounces entirely all the faults of its spiritual past.

Surrender is our complete severance from our old self and an endeavouring to live by God's Guidance as one with Christ. Life-changing is not idealistic clap-trap—as some doubters would term it—but an absolutely true change, the wonder of the results of which are provable beyond doubt.

Surrendering our lives to God means a complete giving back to God of the will-power He gave us at Creation which, with the Ages, has separated itself by Sin from the Giver, and our taking, in its place, His will as He intended our will should be when He first made man in His own image.

Will-power is acknowledged to be an active force, as positive in its effects as, for example, electricity; these effects and their extensions are beyond our present knowledge; we only know that the will-power has been the driving force for the actual accomplishment of great works, deeds, feats, and inventions, and that if the will-power behind them is sufficient seemingly impossible things can be carried to completion. The will-power for the accomplishment of great achievements in the past has come from God; the will-power of our generation, if it be put under God-Direction, has boundless possibilities; surrendering our wills to God does not mean that our faculties are thereby deadened but that they are awakened with the infinite power of God behind them and with the direction of His judgement for their best use—according to the individual Plan He has mapped out for each of us.

Our surrender to God should be so complete that 'In Him we live, we move, and have our being' should be actual. This is not a dream we should like to think possible if we had the spiritual strength or the visionary powers of some of the Saints to make it so. If we surrender our lives to God with Absolute Honesty and immediately commence to rely with Absolute Love on His Guidance for the future direction of our surrendered lives, it is a possible state for all of us. This is such a simple fact that it appears intricate to some—as simple facts sometimes do. But, in spite of its sounding simplicity, Surrender is one of the few things in our lives which cannot be done for us; a proxy cannot stand for us. It is an act that can only be performed by the individual; there exists no religious rite, qualifying condition, or expediency which could take its place. It is our individual Surrender to God revealed in Christ. Long prayers, excuses for our past, licence asked for the future, are not of the least use; to God who knows each one of us far better than we could ever know ourselves, the spirit is of far more importance than the letter. We either do or do not surrender. As far as the act itself is concerned that is all there is to it.

Repent ye therefore, and turn again that your sins may be blotted out, so that there may come seasons of refreshing from the presence of the Lord.

The word 'converted' is much despised amongst us moderns.

It savours of religious hysteria, dramatic penitent-form scenes—which serve a very useful purpose for those whom only such scenes can awaken to a living Christ—old-fashioned British revivalism or the latest American religious fervour. But the word conversion itself, although not in habitual use by the Oxford Group, is a good one and there is no reason why, if it is our idea of surrender, any of us who want to use it should refrain from doing so. But Absolute Surrender to God, as seen by the Oxford Group, is conversion with a definite constructive spiritual policy added which ensures it being of positive use and fertility for us and for others. Like conversion, Surrender needs repentance, a realization that our lives are out of harmony with Christ, a determination to live better spiritual lives and our complete conviction that God can, and will, take from us all our sins and make our future as if our past had never been; but in addition Surrender needs our sure and certain conviction that when we are 'converted' and God takes over our lives He will Guide them and we shall feel that refreshing state of living which shall come with the presence of the Lord within us.

Quite a number of us quarrel over the use of a certain word to describe a situation or an act, and to some Surrender is the wrong word to use for the Changing, or the 'conversion', of our lives from world direction to God Direction. We visualize Surrender as a showing of the white flag, the confessing of defeat to an enemy more powerful than ourselves and the asking for a truce, perhaps at any costs. To those of us who think like that, Surrender is then definitely a weak and cowardly action. We say we would rather go on, like tried and proved trusty soldiers, to the end and then pay the cost, if any, that is coming to us. Capitulation never was and never will be in our fighting code; we have never, we say, laid down our arms to an enemy, and never will. But, if any of you others because you are not strong enough to live your own lives like real men want to get support for your weaknesses, go ahead and get it if it gives you any pleasure or satisfaction. Only leave *us* out of your Surrender to God business, please!

How fine those of us who talk and think like that feel! We really think of God as a far-away fault-finding Deity whose demands, if we gave in to Him or took too much notice of Him, would make life, which is already difficult enough, almost unbearable. It is strange, although we may not always put it in so many words, how many of us think on these lines. It is not surprising, therefore, that those who have this conception of God take submission to Him to signify a cowardly act when, all the time, it is a courageous decision to do a courageous thing. It wants little or no courage to be a self-centered sinner, proud of independence and self-will. It needs a tremendous amount of courage to die to the world in which are the very roots of our being and to live in Christ to the best of our spiritual ability. The courage of those who resign their lives to God is not the kind of courage understood by those who find fault with the word Surrender. It is spiritual courage which, possible to every man and every woman, means the sacrifice of our confidence and our pride in the material ego. Only those who have surrendered know that it does not mean cringing or apologizing but joining, with courageous optimism, Christ and our brother Christians in spiritual fellowship.

Our initial Surrender to God does not mean that henceforth we shall be asleep to the world around us; that temptations will never assail nor sins conquer us again, and that, if they do, God is not living up to His part of the compact: or that, because we are not strong enough to carry out our Guidance as really good Christians, it is hopeless to think that we can continue to live under God's Direction.

It means that after Surrender we have to work and eat and sleep and laugh and play as before, and that in the round of daily life come situations which cause reactions against our spiritual good resolutions. It would be foolish for any of us to pretend that human nature is otherwise; Sin remains Sin, but even if we only surrendered to God yesterday our sin of to-day does not cancel that surrender. God knows and waits. He waits to see if we will Surrender that sin of to-day to Him with as much sincerity as we surrendered our lives yesterday; to see if we will acknowledge it was lack of trust that made us fail to ask Him to take that sin away from us while it was still temptation; to see if we will confess that it was want of faith in His Guidance that made us vulnerable to spiritual weakness.

Many 'converted' lose heart very quickly; and say they are not strong enough to carry out what they may call their 'Good Resolution'. But if we believe in surrender that excuse is nonsense. Our lives will be one continuous surrender: surrender to God of every difficulty that confronts us, each temptation, each spiritual struggle; laying them before Him either to take away or to show to us in their proper spiritual proportions. Continuous submission of our difficulties to God is not weakness, as some of us may imagine. Temptations to saints do not stop, nor are they less tempting than to sinners. None of us may ever be saints, but that is no reason why we should not be sensible sinners.

The Oxford Group recommend our making the initial act of Surrender to God in the presence of another person who is already a Changed Life, or in the presence of a person who has for some time been an active Christian. In this wise advice lies the knowledge that a witness is a help to us to make our Surrender complete in the sight of God and Man; that like the oaths we take for mundane affairs the witness's signature is often as valuable as the testator's.

The presence of a Christian witness should not be an embarrassment to us; rather should it be an outward sign of our intention to join a fellowship of surrendered lives among men, joining hands with that fellowship at the same moment as the direction of our lives goes out of our individual keeping into the hands of God.

The Oxford Group initial act of Surrender is not, in any way, an outward and visible ceremony we feel we must shrink from; it is a simple decision put into simple language, spoken aloud to God, in front of a witness, at any time and in any place, that we have decided to forget the past in God and to give our future into His keeping. Nothing more need be added; nothing can be taken away.

The Lord's Prayer is a perfect example of Surrender to God; for Christ, in its composition, gave us in the shortest number of essential phrases the essentials of complete submission to His Father. If we have doubts about the Surrender to God used by the Oxford Group we should say the Lord's Prayer to ourselves, dwelling on and thinking out the complete and absolute meaning of each word and phrase with direct application to ourselves. If we are busy people we can take only two or three minutes over each word or phrase, but we could continue to discover in Christ's simple Prayer of Surrender limitless meanings and implications we never thought existed. It is a masterpiece which sums up who God is, where He is, His attitude to us, and what our attitude should be to Him.

The essential point in studying the Lord's Prayer as Surrender in its complete form is to ask ourselves if we really are convinced that we believe in and act on each phrase in our daily lives. To take the simplest example, do we believe absolutely that God is 'Our Father'?—not only in the spiritual sense of the word but in our responsibilities to Him as our Creator? If we are convinced of this, are we living our spiritual and material lives based on those two words? Do we frankly acknowledge God is our Father to the world, or do we, because we are afraid of ridicule or not sure if its practical significance would work for our advantage in our daily lives, just treat it as two words in a prayer? How many of us live our lives according to the simple logic that as God is our Father we are all one family and all men are really brothers of Christ? Or do we say to ourselves: 'That sounds very excellent and idealistic on paper or in the pulpit and we like to think it is true, but is it a possible working worldly hypothesis?' Do many of us realize that if those few who govern us would believe and act on these two simple words God's Plan for the world could speedily come into action and the future, which is more serious than any of us can conceive in the present world chaos, would be assured for universal happiness and content?

'Thy will be done' are the four little words that give us the crux to the surrender of our will-power which is usually the last thing we wish to surrender to God. How many of us say daily to God 'Thy will be done—not mine. Thy Will shall be my will; I surrender to You that puny will of mine which I thought was my individual property and which, being of the earth, fails me when I most need it or causes me to lead a life of Self-worship'? Who amongst us can say that in Absolute Honesty not only when we pray the Lord's Prayer but every time we come up against a problem in our lives?

The Oxford Group finds that desire and decision to make this Surrender do not come at any recognized or pre-arranged time in a life. Through desire for conversion, effected by witness heard from other Changed lives, some decide to surrender themselves very quickly; some, although wishing to make the change, take a prolonged time to come to a decision because they have honest doubts as to the definite necessity for that change in their lives; others are frankly mistrustful and doubt Christ's Power or are dubious of the effect a surrendered life may have on their immediate material existence.

The first impressions some people have of the Oxford Group are anything but flattering. They mistrust the outspokenness of the Group; dislike their direct methods of dealing with Sin; have criticisms which seem at the time to them to have foundations of truth. Some unchanged people who go to Oxford Group meetings and House-parties look for the 'nigger in the woodpile' and, when they cannot find him, hate the woodpile. Why? Mainly because they suspect other people of having faults they definitely have themselves, and because direct discussion on spiritual matters impels them immediately to look for ulterior motives; when they fail to find these they fall back on abuse. In some sinners this attitude is very natural. It is their particular form of Sin, and, Sin being what it is, it is not to be wondered at if they go into paroxysms of hate and destructive criticism.

But these scoffers do not deter the Oxford Group, whose message is to sinners of all grades and kinds. It looks upon its critics in the only normal Christian way—as excellent material for life changing; and it is a remarkable fact that many of these scoffers, in spite of their abuse and suspicion, often return to Oxford Group gatherings drawn—although they do not put it exactly like that—by a power stronger than themselves, the truth of Christ, and when they are Changed, as some of them eventually are, they become as progressive for the Group as they were formerly critical.

'I have learned, in whatsoever state I am, therein to be content,' wrote St. Paul.

The Oxford Group knows for certain that this is the state of life of those who are surrendered to God. It is the only contentment that withstands the urgings and promptings of the world towards the illusion of undue material gain and of those things which are ambitious for pomps and vanities. It is a perfectly balanced state; normal in outlook and in progression. There is nothing of fanaticism or fatalism about it. It is complete trust in the absolute belief that whatsoever is good to us or a trial to us, whether it be joy or sorrow, plenty or little, love or hate, can be all turned to good account in God's service; and whatever lot God appoints to be best for us is the best we can choose for ourselves. The state of contentment St. Paul knew is not an idle or weak effortless life in which we can sit back and do nothing. It is the result of an active spiritual life which is just as possible for us moderns to live fully as in St. Paul's time. There is no one and nothing in this modern world, of which many of us are the discontented products, to prevent us from relinquishing our lives to God; those of us who think there is put too much value on ourselves. To keep it from becoming more and more unbalanced Civilization to-day needs millions of surrendered lives. Passive Christians are no more entitled to ignore the active spiritual fruits of their potential Surrender to God than they would be in keeping back any material discovery that would benefit the world at large.

None of us know who are the key-people of the world's future. The results of the Surrender of one life may mean a world change towards Christ and an ultimate universal state of contentment. We cannot predict what any single surrendered life is capable of accomplishing. Those who are nominal Christians only and who have not contemplated surrendering to God but have the problems of the world at heart, are ignoring, either through pride or self-worship, a practical opportunity to make a real contribution to world betterment; and those who are practising Christians and cannot, because of lack of faith, use the abundance of power which God has put into their hands, are ignoring the fact that God can use everybody for the good of their fellow men. Even the most inarticulate or humble of us can assist Him to work out to fruitful completion some little but important corner of His World Plan.

RESTITUTION

'To them that love God
all things work together for good.'
ROMANS VIII. 28.

'What is past is past.
There is a future left to all men
who have the virtue to repent
and energy to atone.'
LORD LYTTON.

RESTITUTION

'Repent ye therefore, and turn again,
that your sins may be blotted out.'
—ACTS III. 19.

IN these days we moderns believe tremendously in what
we see more than in what we hear. We want concrete facts
not theories. There is no time to dally with fine-
sounding idealisms or to spend much of what we believe is
'precious' time listening to long sermons, as did our forefathers.
We want action; action with palpable results that are obvious to
everybody. Modern reason and doubt are influenced by the material. 'Show us!' is our cry. Everything comes under that demand.
We want results about the spiritual as well as the material. We
must be convinced.

'Wisdom is the principal thing; therefore get wisdom: yea,
with all thou hast gotten get understanding', we are told in
Proverbs. It is little use us getting the wisdom of what God's
power and guidance can mean in our lives, to Surrender to God
and attempt to live a changed life, if that wisdom does not show
us that it is absolutely essential that we should get understanding with those we love, work with or come in contact with in our
daily lives; and we cannot get that understanding with them
unless we are honest about our wrong thoughts and actions in
connexion with them. Restitution is openly cutting the cord of
sin which has bound us to the life of wrong we have lived in
the past, and the only way of doing this is by acknowledging
our faults to the people concerned and to pay back by apology or

in kind if necessary that which we have taken from them. Whatever it is, important or seemingly unimportant, we are debtors and must pay now that our lives are God's, and it is definitely not only a question of 'owning up' but, to confirm the cancellation of the debt we owe, of making concrete restitution.

Restitution is righting to the best of our present ability wrongs we have committed in the past. The reception given to our acts of restitution by those to whom we make them are, in themselves, an interesting sidelight on human character. Often because we are honest, and frankly acknowledge a sin to the person we have wronged by it, that person is awakened to the realization of what a Changed Life may mean to him or her; and our act of restitution not only brings forgiveness with it but a new life to God. Only ill-timed atonement might cause harm; nearly always atonement, by sheer honesty, brings us new friends or a better understanding with our old friends. The Absolute Honesty of restitution is usually a new wonder to those who have been until then unaware of what a surrendered life can mean in a world where dishonesty is often taken for granted and truth has lost much of its meaning.

To strangers to the Oxford Group, Changed Lives, unless they have something concrete to show for that change, are not in themselves evidence of spiritual reawakening, and in these days to make people who doubt sit up and take notice of anything that is not entirely of the earth, changed folk must be concrete. Changed ways of living, changed outlook, and changed attitude towards our fellow men, are essentially part of Changed Lives, but restitution is the one thing that often causes unchanged people to rub their eyes and wonder if a new phenomenon, the exact nature of which they cannot define, has come into their world, making them either feel that the universe is growing even madder or that it is becoming very sane.

Confronted by a Changed person who comes to make restitution for some wrong done, many unchanged people are not sure how to deal with the situation. Some one coming, seemingly out of the blue, to make, with Absolute Honesty and humility, restitution for a wrong done to them! It is unprecedented; and there are no printed rules or regulations they can refer to which will tell them how, without loss of dignity or acquiring patronage, to deal with this strange situation; and, more important than that, there is obviously no ulterior motive in the amazing visit of this Changed Life which has come to them voluntarily to confess, ask forgiveness and, if the wrong demands it, to repay. That, in itself, is unique and is not to be dealt with by reference to any book of words.

As they listen to this Changed Life which suddenly confronts them these strangers to restitution often do not understand the feelings they experience. Yes, the world, they are quite certain, is becoming very mad—or, perhaps, very, very sane!

They would be surprised, these people, if the Oxford Group told them that, when confronted with a Changed Life making restitution to them, their mixed feelings are due not to men or women talking about wrong and right but to the unusual situation of one soul facing another with Absolute Honesty and with Christ as witness. There is little wonder that from a worldly point of view restitution appears as a phenomenon and that, more often than not, they can use no words of condemnation or of ridicule, for often during our restitution to others God speaks to them about themselves.

Those who have surrendered and made complete atonement for their wrongs to other people are in agreement that they have never, whatever the cost has been to them, regretted making the right sort of restitution. It often requires more courage than some of us can imagine ourselves possessing to make a confession which might very conceivably spell ruin in the eyes of society; but those who wish to put themselves right with God know they must also put themselves right with man; and so a husband tells a wife of a sin which has been the cause of their drifting apart; a confession goes to some one too far off to own up to by spoken word and atones for a wrong; an employer is interviewed by an employee who acknowledges some wrong done against him and vice versa; sins are acknowledged, forgiveness asked. But whatever the occasion of the restitution, it is not just an empty dramatic gesture with no true or constructive significance; it is an indispensable condition for the birth of a new spiritual life.

Restitution is not easy. Only those who have done so realize the strength sometimes needed to write even a letter of restitution to a person thousands of miles away as atonement for a sin, even though that sin may be known only to the writer. It may be a sin that might never come to light but for the letter of restitution; or a sin that appears trivial to the world; perhaps we have been dishonest or uncharitable only in thought. But, without God's positive power behind us, a letter about what may seem to strangers a trivial matter, but one which will get us right with ourselves and men, is often difficult even to place in the post-box. So we stand cogitating on the possible effects of slipping that letter in that post-box and allowing it to fall to where we can never retrieve it. Doubting God, a wave of self-consciousness comes over us, a feeling that we may be making fools of ourselves unnecessarily, lowering our prestige, asking for trouble; a conviction that the unconfessed past is the past and is best forgotten. But if while we hesitate we realize that God is really with us and that an act of restitution, great or small as it may be, is necessary, our hand, God guided, without hesitation creeps up to the post-box and the letter goes beyond our recalling, to carry out one more act of atonement that will set us free from our past selves.

John Roots in his challenging Oxford Group pamphlet *An Apostle to Youth* describes very helpfully what restitution even by letter writing can mean to an unhappy soul. Writing of Frank Buchman he says:

> '. . . he accepted the pastorate of a church among the
> working people of Philadelphia, leaving this charge at the end
> of three years to found the first Lutheran hospice and settle-
> ment house for poor boys. A difference with the trustees led to

*his resignation in protest at what he considered their insuf-
ficient provision of food for the boys, and in 1908 he again
went abroad. He was unhappy and perplexed. Resentment
against certain of the trustees festered in his heart. For some
time he had had an uneasy feeling that this was causing the
trouble. Always pride had forbidden humiliation before these
men against whom he felt he had a just grievance.*

'*Whilst visiting in the English Lake District and still in
this state of mind he wandered one day into a little country
church where a woman was speaking on some aspect of the
Cross. Something in what she said stirred him to the depths,
and he saw himself for what he truly was. It was the turning-
point. Next day he mailed to America six letters of simple
apology, and at the head of each he wrote:*

When I survey the wondrous Cross

On which the Prince of Glory died,

My richest gain I count but loss,

And pour contempt on all my pride.

*He never heard from those six men. But for the first
time in a year he felt the power of Christ returning as an
inward reality.*'

'And pour contempt on all my pride'! That is the secret not
only of restitution but of a spiritual life. What great unimaginable possibilities it conjures up for us! If we could pour contempt on all our pride there is no avenue of spiritual life which
would not be open to us. There is nothing we would hesitate to
do to put ourselves right with God and man. Self would go by the
board and in its place a great understanding would come.
Restitution would be the perfect God-guided act for our ultimate
spiritual perfection, not only when we initially change our lives
to Christ but throughout the difficulties of our striving for a

spiritual life. How many of us can pour contempt on all our pride—not fifty per cent. but a hundred per cent. of it? Or how many realize what that contempt would mean to us? It would not be just ignoring our pride but spurning it as if it were something far too inferior to our natures to be noticed.

'When Pride cometh, then cometh Shame', is what the proverb says, and pride enters into many more things we think, say, or do than we realize. Even in making restitution pride tries hard to take a hand. 'Shall I bother to tell the authorities that I did something which was the cause of So-and-So getting into trouble, although he was innocent?' a man contemplating restitution says to himself. 'If I confess now it may mean losing all my friends, having to leave the town, being laughed at for raking up a silly scandal which died down years ago; being made to feel small and ridiculous for not leaving well alone. Anyway, if I do confess, I feel I shall never be able to lift up my head again.' And so pride goes on, giving us what appear to be good excuses for not making atonement for some sin which lies hidden from man, but not from God, when, if we could be honest with ourselves and pour contempt on all our pride, we should realize that this very act of restitution is absolutely necessary, whatever the cost, if we are to right an injustice to another and put ourselves right with God.

'What if my restitution towards a certain person does more harm than good?' Some of us, with good excuse, often ask that. The answer is that where it is essential the important thing for us is to go through with restitution, for none of us knows for certain what effect our acts of atonement will have until we have made them. The results of restitution are often so unexpectedly in our favour that we wonder afterwards why we had any qualms about making it.

Into this problem there enters the important solution of God-guidance. It is the acid test of the good and the wisdom of our intentions and the arbitrator for our decisions. If we remember that surrendered lives are in truth God-directed lives and that we have the Purity of the Christ-mind as our example, prayer can help us where we cannot help ourselves. We are often inclined to forget that God can take care of other people as well as us.

Spiritual discretion is often the better part of mental valour when we contemplate making restitution. It is of no profit to God or man for us to wreck innocent lives by indiscretions prompted by over-zeal. The Holy Spirit is absolute discretion; God-given guidance should prompt all our acts of restitution, telling us what atonement constitutes, the right time to make it, the form it should take, and giving, if we need it, the spiritual strength to carry it out for the best of all parties concerned. There is no knowing the great good our courage will do if it is really God-guided; we may never know how many lives may come to Christ because of it or what it may mean in spiritual gain to us.

Christ gives us, in the Parable of the Prodigal Son, the classic example of restitution. It is always worth repeating:

> "'I will arise", says the Prodigal Son, "and go to my father, and will say unto him, 'Father, I have sinned against heaven, and in thy sight: I am no more worthy to be called thy son: make me as one of thy hired servants.'"
>
> 'And he arose, and came to his father. But while he was yet afar off, his father saw him, and was moved with compassion, and ran, and fell on his neck, and kissed him.
>
> 'And the son said unto him, "Father, I have sinned against heaven, and in thy sight: I am no more worthy to be called thy son."
>
> 'But the father said to his servants, "Bring forth quickly the best robe, and put it on him; and put a ring on his hand, and shoes on his feet: and bring the fatted calf, and kill it; and let us eat, and make merry: for this my son was dead, and is alive again; he was lost, and is found."'

Such is the Divine conception of the act of restitution and there we have in the last sentence Christ's definition of a changed life: '. . . was dead, and is alive again; he was lost and is found.'

It is obvious to us that pride does not enter in this perfect example of atonement. The son makes no excuses for his sins. He shoulders them and faces his father; he is simple, direct, and honest. That is exactly what our restitution should be, although it may be misunderstood by those who hear the rejoicing but do not know the cause, for Christ shows us that some people are unable to comprehend restitution and forgiveness when in the parable the elder son, who has heard his father's rejoicing at the younger son's return, complains to his father, reminding him of his good service that has received none such reward. The father replies to the elder son's protests by again saying: 'For this my son was dead, and is alive again; he was lost, and is found.' That is the perfect description of a changed life. It is inevitable that unless we can make them understand all that restitution means to a changed life there will be people of the elder son type always with us.

We must not expect all our acts of restitution to be received with acclamations of joy as if we are all prodigal sons returning home, and should therefore receive the modern equivalent of a fatted calf. Our atonement may perhaps mean payment that will be a trial to us, or it may be flatly ignored as were Frank Buchman's six letters. But if we make our restitution in the right spirit it is certain that we shall know that 'power of Christ as an inward reality'.

G UIDANCE

'*But as it is written, Things which eye saw not,*
and ear heard not, and which entered not
into the heart of man, whatsoever things God
prepared for them that love Him.'

1 CORINTHIANS II. 9.

'*For as many as are led*
by the Spirit of God,
these are sons of God.'

ROMANS VIII. 14.

GUIDANCE

'For we walk by faith, not by sight.'
—2 COR. V. 7.

*D*IVINE guidance to a life changed from Sin to God is
the Holy Spirit taking a normal intelligence and
directing it in the fullest harmony with His will for the
good of the individual and his neighbours.

Seeming trivialities are not overlooked by the Holy Spirit. A
small point overlooked to-day may have a big consequence to-
morrow. Suggestions as to conduct, solutions to material and
spiritual difficulties are given by daily guidance. It is God using
for our best, in partnership with us, the lives we have surrendered
to His care.

The Oxford Group realize that guidance is not anyone's
particular property; it is as free to all of us as are the sun and air,
and that there is no reason why every one, whatever their status
or Christian creed, cannot come out of the darkness to breathe
the clear and spiritual health-giving properties of God's radiant
counsel. 'Every good gift and every perfect boon is from above.'
Life under guidance takes on eventful potentialities, is full of
interest, and is in accordance with every type of personality. It is
all-wise and all-embracing, building up our right God-appointed
kind of ego, until we feel that life has always for us in the future
that adventurous feeling of youth and hope that is reborn within
most of us when on a glorious fresh morning we breathe the
exhilarating air of Spring.

Divine guidance takes away from us that fear of to-morrow

which, in conjunction with the troubles of to-day, so often makes life intolerable for us. Not only is our to-day in God's keeping but our to-morrow; we have surrendered that to Him, too, so why fear whatever we think to-morrow must bring us as a logical sequence of to-day's events? Fear of the future, whether it be to-morrow or old age, means that we do not trust in God's guidance. Our faith in the future is the infallible test of our faith in Him. How many people have it? Can we visualize half the world or even our few friends free from fear not only of the present but of the future? If this could be, unbalanced civilization would slow down to its proper course, like a stream that has battled its way through rocks and crevices and reached, at long last, a smooth, straight course, where the sunlight ripples through its crystal clearness, as it flows serenely on to meet the Great Ocean we call the After-Life.

A Quiet Time with the Holy Spirit every morning before 'the daily toil and common round' of the world commences will put us in the right key for the day. These early morning Quiet Times in which God impresses on our minds His counsel become living spots in the routine of ordinary life. The Oxford Group advocates our use of a pencil and note-book so that we may record every God-given thought and idea that comes to us during our time alone with Him, that no detail, however small, may be lost to us and that we may not shirk the truth about ourselves or any problem, when it comes to us.

It is not suggested that everything we write down during our Quiet Times necessarily comes from God. The human mind, being what it is, wanders from concentration at an outside interruption, takes up a train of thought it finds hard to discard, invents or remembers a thought of its own. But to those closely in touch with God it becomes easy after a short while to differentiate between spiritual and human messages. In cases of difficulty our guidance can be 'checked up' with the teachings of the Bible or by conference with others who are also receiving guidance in Quiet Times.

Prayer is the natural complement of God Direction. We cannot expect God to talk to us if we do not talk to Him, but to the Oxford Group it is not always essential continually to ask God for help in every move we make, or in every problem of our daily lives. If we have faithfully surrendered our lives to Him, God is our Pilot and knows our every movement and thought. When we listen for His guidance during our Quiet Times all requests asked or unasked are answered. Petitions are not always necessary, for if our attitude towards God is conducive to real guidance, then that in itself is Prayer.

The age of miracles is still with us, although we may not see the signs in the sky or the spectacular manifestations on earth which we think miracles are. Real prayer receives a real answer in any place at any time. 'God works in a mysterious way His wonders to perform' in a world that confuses the material shadow with the spiritual substance. No supplication to God from the heart is ever lost. We may think the answer to it is a long time coming or that it is not answered in the way we want, but to God, who knows neither Space nor Time, it is the best answer at the best time for us. *For a thousand years in Thy sight are but as yesterday when it is past, and as a watch in the night.*

Words in every language, spoken aloud or mentally formed, in sincere prayer are active spiritual messages radiating to God and received by Him as soon as they are uttered. Prayer does not depend on an attitude of the physical body but on the attitude of the spiritual self. Neither does prayer, of necessity, bring a feeling of spiritual elevation nor does its reality depend on the form or the wording our petitions take. Fixed forms of prayer used in services are necessary for united worship, and written prayers emanating from God-fearing men and women are real aids to our closer communion with God. But neither a Church nor a saintly composer of the most beautiful prayer would suggest that the fixed prayer is more than a guide to the prayer we should pray when we are alone with God.

It is necessary in our Quiet Times to give our minds to God

free from doubts and distractions, to ensure our absolute negation to everything but our conviction that He can, and will, tell
us what He thinks best for us to do, or not to do, in the plan of
our daily lives, or in a problem which confronts us. If we truly
believe our guidance is from God we must recognize that it is not
necessary to ask God numberless times for His help in a difficulty
or to agitate ourselves lest He should fail us in His answer. 'Use
not vain repetitions', said St. Matthew.

The Reverend R. H. Steuart, S.J., in his helpful little essay
A Map of Prayer gets down, with real human insight, to the difficulties the average person has in shutting himself or herself
entirely away from the world when in prayer:

> *'Distractions', he writes, 'may be divided roughly into two
> kinds: (1) Thoughts about one's daily activities, past, present,
> and future; associations called up by sounds and movements
> around us; definite temptations of every description, coming
> one knows not whence. (2) Weariness, with accompanying
> disgust for our present occupation; doubts about the prayer
> itself; fears of idleness, self-delusion, vanity; strong impulses
> to get up at once and do something else—this, often, just
> when our sensible devotion is at its strongest. These are often,
> too, intensified by secret doubts about the forgiveness of past
> sin, and clouded by an indefinable feeling that somehow I am
> radically different, for the worse, from every one else, and that,
> do what I may, I never shall and never can get nearer to God.'*

Prayer and Quiet Times with God are very similar in the
various distractions and doubts which often beset them. When
a God-thought comes into our minds we sometimes doubt its
authenticity; we say to ourselves, 'It's all very well to get that as
guidance, but what is the use of it to me without the practical
means to carry it out?' It is then that we are forgetting that God
never guides us to do anything He does not give us the means to
carry out. 'Faith is the assurance of things hoped for, the proving
of things not seen.' If we trust and go right ahead to carry out His

instructions, however obscure the means or objective may seem to us, it is amazing to the unenlightened minds how God not only provides the guidance but the assistance and the outcome which is best for us according to His Plan. Doubt stifles and makes abortive our attempt to act upon God-Counsel. When we carry out fearlessly God-given prompting to do what may seem at the moment impossible in our circumstances, we see the Divine meaning and implication of Christ's walking on the water—for all time. Christ walked on the water to show us that by faith everything is possible. He walked that water trusting in God. It was His demonstration to men of the powers of Faith. According to our faith is it possible unto us, was His message.

Self-will is the hardest thing in existence to surrender to God. The majority of us will surrender just enough of ourselves to Him so that we can keep what we think is our independence. It is that little piece of self-will we keep, even although we think it is so secret and hidden that God Himself will not notice it, which prevents us from receiving the infinite and complete benefits and grace of guidance. We must give our entirety to God in our Quiet Times with Him and when we are carrying His guidance out. This seems at first as difficult as is giving one's entire thoughts and concentration to God in prayer, but discipline over our self-will, although it may be slow, comes with practice; and practice and regularity are as necessary to learning to make the best use of guidance as they are in learning anything that is worth learning in this world.

THE FOUR ABSOLUTES

1 . ABSOLUTE HONESTY

'*Whatsoever things are true, whatsoever things are honourable,*
whatsoever things are just, whatsoever things are pure,
whatsoever things are lovely,
whatsoever things are of good report;
if there be any virtue, and if there be any praise,
think on these things.'

PHILIPPIANS IV. 8.

'*Live pure, speak true,*
right wrong, follow the King –
Else, wherefore born?'

TENNYSON.

'*All things are possible to him who believes;*
they are less difficult to him who hopes;
they are easy to him who loves,
and simple to any one who do all three.'

BROTHER LAURENCE.

ABSOLUTE HONESTY

'Bright Thoughts, clear Deeds,
Constancy, Fidelity, Bounty
and generous Honesty
are the gems of noble minds.'
SIR THOMAS BROWNE.

'To thine own self be true,' said Shakespeare, 'and it must follow as the night the day thou canst not then be false to any man.' To ourselves the absolute truth; to others as truthful as we are to ourselves. Can we do it? Can we sit down even for a few moments and face the self the world does not see and tell that self the absolute truth? Then, having told that hidden self the absolute truth, can we be honest and let that truth become a conscious part of ourselves? How many of us can do that?

Absolute honesty is the proud boast of many people. 'One thing about me', they will say, 'is that no one can deny that I'm always honest about everything and everybody.' We all know that complacent type too well. They enjoy pointing out other people's weaknesses and indiscretions to their face and are rather surprised when the recipients of this form of honesty are not exactly pleased. Why on earth should other people be pleased when we destroy their illusions or lay bare their weak points? The methods of the self-righteous, who would be honest at all costs but their own, are more harmful to spiritual life than they realize and bring contempt on the work of Christ. 'A conscience void of offence toward God and men' is the best remedy for self-righteous honesty.

Under God's guidance absolute truthfulness is tempered with common sense and kindliness. There is no reason why we should flaunt and enjoy what we think is Absolute Honesty so much that we should tell a neighbour a truth about himself which is neither a sin of his nor our business. Striving for Absolute Honesty should not be a weapon for us to bludgeon our way to what we think is perfection. 'Love thy neighbour as thyself' is sufficient test as to our motives for honesty. There is no reason why, in our determination to be honest with God, we should destroy the belief in God in other people; and many people's belief in God is founded on their belief in humanity, kindliness, faithfulness, in the fulfillment of obligations, moral or material. God-given discretion is better than our unloving determination to be honest at all costs, mostly other people's.

'An honest man's the noblest work of God', quotes Robert Burns. Honesty must be allied to nobility of mind and purpose. Some of us use frankness as a sort of scourge to punish those we feel are not quite as good as we think we are. Minds such as these are farther from Christ than they suppose. Is honesty that has no discretion much use? St. Paul says: 'All things are lawful; but all things are not expedient. All things are lawful; but all things edify not.' Honesty is the truth which belongs to God, and when we use it we are using God's power. If we use God's power in the wrong way or at the wrong time, why should we grumble because it is ineffective or has the opposite effect to what we think it should have? A sudden fit of frankness about other people without a preliminary self-examination can do untold harm. We must be absolutely honest with ourselves before we can be absolutely honest about other people. It is one of the essentials of Christian life.

Many people revel in what they think is Absolute Honesty. They are convinced that it means telling the bald, unvarnished facts about themselves even if it involves other people. If the truth is without consideration or discretion, it is better to keep a silent tongue and await the decision of our guidance than to blurt out what may be a truth but a truth which will send a person even farther from leading a Christian life. God-given counsel is wise counsel. Petty criticisms do not induce a vital faith in God. Truth should not be merely destructive but spiritually constructive. Honesty is not, of necessity, criticism. If Love is the rock from which our fountain of Honesty springs, then it is Honesty in its purest sense.

Family life must have its roots in honesty if the family is to remain united. It is not surprising that children who know that their parents are not honest with each other are not honest with their parents. Modern children are said by some popular writers to be an unsolvable problem, a kind of phenomenon in the social history of the world. Children of any age are a problem to the grown-ups of a previous generation and they always will be. Modern children are products of modern conditions and as they grow with it have to adapt themselves to the changing conditions of the world. It is not the fault of the modern children that a large percentage of them are happy-go-lucky pagans who have discarded God as an out-of-date institution. Their eyes are naturally eagerly fixed on the promised fruits of life, vitality and progress. If their parents or their teachers cannot, or will not, show the power of Christ to youth as a living force which does not bind youth but offers it the best and fullest way of living, then the fault is theirs, because they will not face the undeniable truth that the simple rules of Christianity are as modern, and as applicable to enjoyment and appreciation of life as its best to-day as they were when Christ changed the old tribal conditions into a new and practical way of family co-operation.

Honesty in morals is an essential to a real happiness which has no fear of the present or the future. How can any husband or wife live in perfect understanding if either has a secret which, should it come to light from an outside source, will wreck their partnership? If real, unshakable love exist between two people, whatever the fault that one may confess to the other, it will sink into insignificance, or take its proper place between them, if honesty is made as a tribute to that love. A sin which comes to light from an outside source often destroys the union of two people. Reluctance to be honest about our faults, mistakes, or sins with a person we are united to by love is lack of faith, not only in that person but also in the reality of that love. A love which dies because one confesses, with honest motives, a sin to the other is not worth having, and any love which can embrace mutual honesty is very near to the ideal which God had for men and women when He ordained marriage.

Moral honesty with our friends, who co-operate with us for happiness, is very necessary if we are to know that we can rely on them to stand with us in an emergency. How much more do we value friends whose affection is founded on candour and who will be honest with us when we are confronted with difficult situations in which we need honesty if we are to set a right view-point. What are the use of half-truths, vapid words of consolation, or negative advice to us when we are facing a crisis which needs to be confronted with Absolute Honesty? Some of us are like the proverbial ostrich which hides its head in the sand. How often do we say, 'If it's anything unpleasant I don't want to hear it!' when subconsciously we know that the best thing for us would be to face the truth honestly and seek for an honest solution to our problem or our sin. We cannot always hide our heads in the sands of the fallacy that ignorance is bliss; our heads have to come out sometimes, and we often find that whilst we have been shutting our eyes to it the truth has grown much more difficult to cope with. Friendship that will allow for honest facing of mutual difficulties is the only kind of friendship which is worth our having; the mutual ostrich kind is hardly friendship; it certainly is not honest.

How any one can possibly be even apparently honest in these days, is a question which is very natural. In business to-day, which for most people is one big fight for bare existence, let alone profit, honesty has become a forgotten cypher. Cut-throat competition, false trading representations, underhand methods of salesmanship, lack of capital, worry thousands into premature old age and disillusion. 'Do others before they can do you' is the *motif* of the modern business world. But does it bring lasting fruits to any one? Millionaires' wealth increases even whilst they sleep, but how many millionaires are ever free or can call five minutes of the waking day their own or can have one really free minute alone to face God, to whom money is only the invention of Man and Who recognizes the accumulation of wealth by men as the mirage it is? How many millionaires crash every year from their gilded heights to depths the average man is spared from? Many of us feel we want to be millionaires, and in some aspects it is an understandable ambition, but for every million added to the wealth of one man a million is gained from countless others. The natural wealth of the world is neither ours nor theirs; it is God's. We are all stewards to God, for His property, by His permission. That is a fact no Christian can refute. As that is so, why should we be so ridiculous as to think we can prosper to any real happiness if we use dishonest methods to gain undue possession of the wealth which at its source is Absolute Honesty? The popular belief is that honesty cannot go hand in hand with business. But it can. Many of the Oxford Group who are in business have witnessed to the fact that honesty makes not only for the right kind of business with a just profit but gains them friends, and any astute business man knows that a friend in the business world is a considerable asset. Being honest in business does not mean being a fool. 'Render therefore unto Caesar the things that are Caesar's; and unto God the things that are God's', said Christ.

Absolute Honesty in business means our being level, our playing the game of business as cleanly as we would play any other game. We 'blackball' a man from decent society when he cheats at cards; then how much more should decent society 'blackball' a man who cheats the poor, robs defenseless widows and orphans by his ruthless methods to gain more wealth than he can ever make use of, although his methods of robbery may be within the law? The business world of to-day must be cleaned up, and swiftly, if the devastating moral degeneration its tendencies are causing is to be checked before they have made a lasting harmful impression on the lives of millions.

'Whatsoever ye do, work heartily, as unto the Lord, and not unto men,' said St. Paul. Whatever our work in life, Absolute Honesty can bring it to the only fruition that is worth having. How many of us feel impelled to stop working when the person who oversees us has turned his back? It is a natural inclination but typical of our inborn desire to give only as much as we are compelled to for the wage we are paid. What of those of us who do just the amount of work we need do, in just the way we want to do it, and, although we are paid to give our best, we feel we do not see why we should put ourselves out to give it unless compelled to? Many of us are inclined to forget that unless we give our best in the best possible way and spirit, we cannot expect to get the best either out of our present life or the future. Do we recognize that dishonesty is at the root of our lassitude in the way we perform the work we are paid for? It is spiritually interesting to analyse our working methods and try to discover if we have ever considered Absolute Honesty in any remote way as the due, not only of those we work for, but of Work, which is, in itself, one of the greatest blessings ever bestowed upon mankind.

Some Christian sects spend money, precious time, and talents in proving their exclusive right to be the real and, sometimes, the only true religion, as propounded by Christ. Their statements and reasons for this are mainly honest convictions from good-living people, but how many of these good-living people can face the Absolute Christ. Honesty which would show them that uncompromising Sectarianism has kept more people away from places of worship than it has attracted to them? How many will tell us quite honestly that all that really matters to the world is that Christ should rule where men have failed; how many will confess, in absolute truth, that thousands of clean-living and thinking people prefer to remain spiritually asleep and enjoy the good things of life without religion, because the Christian Faith makes no appeal to them? Will these sects face Absolute Honesty and admit it is not these naturally clean-living people who have failed religion but that it is the religions that have failed them? How many more clergy will join those who have surrendered their lives to God, and witnessed for Christ, and tell us—and, at the same time, God—that they have realized that in their ministries they have taken the letter for the spirit but that henceforth Christ is going to be as real to them as He was to His Disciples? Most clergy are careful in the carrying out of their responsibilities and in their faith; but if they are to bring about the renaissance of Christianity for all, they must recognize Christ, not as a far-away Ideal, but as a close and living Reality.

To us laymen the Oxford Group stresses Absolute Honesty in the practice of our Christianity as of paramount importance, not only to the religions of which we are members, but to the living Faith of Christ the King. How many of us are really living lives of Absolute Sincerity of Christian purpose? Do we really practice on Monday what we have professed on Sunday? Are we in practice soldiers of Christ the King or do we when we sing lustily that we are His Christian soldiers feel stirred for the moment and then desert the ranks directly the hymn has ended? How many of us care whether the place we worship in is empty or full, as long as we are spiritually content and the sermons are not too long? Have we made much, or any, effort to get those outside to come in and to find Christ in our religion or do we think that is the parson's business? Are we *real* Christians? Do we even know the full significance of the word Christian? Is ours a faith we are proud of when we argue about it with an outsider but one which does not make us argue within ourselves whether we are really a good example of the products of that faith? What about the layman's Absolute Honesty? If we expect the clergy to have and practise it we must practise it ourselves.

2 . ABSOLUTE PURITY

'Woe unto you, scribes and Pharisees,
hypocrites! for ye are like unto whited sepulchres,
which outwardly appear beautiful,
but inwardly are full of dead men's bones
and of all uncleanness.'
MATTHEW XXIII. 27.

'Fear to do base, unworthy things, is valour.
If they be done to us — to suffer them is valour, too.'
BEN JONSON.

ABSOLUTE PURITY

'To the pure all things are pure:
but to them that are defiled
and unbelieving nothing is pure;
but both their mind
and their conscience are defiled.
'They profess that they know God;
but by their works
they deny him, being abominable, and disobedient,
and unto every good work reprobate.'
—TITUS I. 15–16.

ABSOLUTE purity is not only a law of Christian life demanding a clean mind in a clean body. It is a much larger word. It embraces clean conduct in business, in work and play, interest in world affairs, our use of our possessions, our attitude towards relations, friends, and acquaintances. In this sense absolute purity is akin to absolute honesty. Purity is being honest to the best side of our natures, mental, physical, and spiritual; it does not of necessity mean dullness. There is adventure in purity.

'Blessed are the pure in heart' said our Lord, and the 'in heart' is the secret of real purity. There is no worse hypocrite than he who is outwardly pure but unpure in his heart, forgetting that although man sees only the man, God sees the soul. All the outward restraint possible is of no significance if the heart festers with impurity. It is typical of some people who pretend to be shocked at some seeming indecency that their own secret thoughts are teeming with indecencies. They arrogate to themselves the external purity of a lovely flower inviting admiration for its exquisite quality of colour and form, but behind the velvet delicacy of its petals is a heart rotten and worm-eaten. When our souls stand naked before God and He sees us in our utter simplicity we face the only test of real purity.

Life to-day revolves round impurity of thought, motives, and conduct. 'Keep moving at all costs!' is the cry that goes up without ceasing day and night. 'Don't stand still or you'll be knocked down and trampled on! Knock the other person down before he can strike a blow at you! He intends to rob you so why not rob him first? . . .

'Newspaper proprietors! Send up the circulation of your papers, and beat your competitors by publishing filth called "Confessions"! Notoriety has a market value! . . . Murderers! Sell your life story for publication to the highest bidder! There's money in it, and you may escape the gallows to enjoy it, if the lawyers haven't taken it for their fees! If you don't escape the gallows you'll have the satisfaction of knowing you'll be remembered for your crime and your confessions for many generations to come! Your name will be a household one and that's better than being a nobody! So advertise! . . .

'You've been divorced several times? Tell the world! The prosaic public like that sort of thing. They'll envy you, and when you marry again they'll talk about your fascination! . . . You drug? Then out with your experiences! Lay bare your soul, your torments, your hideous dreams, and then your name will be billposted throughout the city! When you are taken before the magistrates crowds will fight to get into the court. You'll be featured on the front page of the picture papers! People will stare at you! You'll be in the limelight! Your sins are your salvation from drabness of life! So advertise them! That's Life; and Life's so short and who knows if there's anything after?'

And so the world races round. Publicity which is mistaken for honesty; moral dirt, physical degeneracy, lying, swindling, adultery; they are not impurities the moderns say. In this world where everything is speed and everything is judged by its financial value they are assets. Souls are for sale cheap. No wonder some of us ask how we can possibly live or think purely when the modern paganism of the world makes it impossible! Some say it is silly and a waste of time to try it. Of course it is if we do not know Peace, or want to know it, or do not realize that the Holy Spirit, for the temptations that the Power of Christ takes away, gives back in return real happiness and constructive consolation a thousandfold. The Pure in Heart do not only see God but hear Him. They know that Absolute Purity is never in vain.

Sex is the word that either makes people pretend to shudder at its sound and the thought of its implications or makes them sit up and take notice. In the mind of many people sex still remains a rather sordid invention of Nature that is best not spoken of at any time, let alone discussed openly. To others continence is impossible, sex is their all-in-all; their world that revolves round it and all its trappings. Sex is love to them; the vitality in an otherwise humdrum world. They earn money for it; dress for it; live for it and dream of it; without this blatant absorbing sex-obsession they can conceive no life possible for them; everything they do is traceable to sex-domination. Impurity? 'What is that?' they ask. There is no such word as impurity to those people who have made sex their god.

Those others who deliberately put sex beyond the pale of discussion and consign it to the darkness of ignorance are often dangerous sinks of impurity themselves. Their whispers are even more destructive than the voices that shout sex from the housetops. Their veiled innuendoes and allusions to sex often bring a blush to the cheek of the normal person more readily than a healthy allusion to sex, when that allusion is in its natural place. Impurity is the reason for these whisperings, not the purity those people delude themselves it is, and impurity which is disguised as purity is impurity of the most harmful kind.

In the education of the young sex is still a bone of contention; many elders still believe the young can be brought up as better Christians if they are spoon-fed on fairy stories about their origin. They would rather let their children as they grow to adolescence invent ghastly mental pictures or develop a horror of sex as something unclean, than put sex on a normal basis for instruction when the young mind is in a receptive condition to be put wise to natural instincts and methods of propagation. Those parents and teachers who are incapable of or shudder at the thought of enlightening a young mind which needs, at an opportune moment in its life, a simple helpful explanation of sex, are suffering from a shame which has its roots deep in impurity. 'To the pure all things are pure', and the minds of the normal young receive sex instruction, helpfully given by one they respect, with the purity and reverence that is its natural right.

With certain sets of people who call themselves 'Intellectuals' impurity has become the fashion. A number of these 'Intellectuals' are really mental snobs with minds that, of little use to any one, are filled with colossal impertinence. Writers of a certain class of fiction decry all forms of decency and purity, gulling by their sheer audacity the reading public into the belief that if they put expressions and words that are not usually used in decent society into print it is a sign of genius. Writers who have been given by God talents beyond the ordinary descend into depths of filth in their work that would make the average hard-swearing but honest man disgusted. Even if literary critics condemn a pornographic book for its blatant indecency the sales do not suffer; publicity of any kind is an advertisement and there is an enormous number of people who will rush to buy a book which has been condemned for its indecency or, should the work be banned from public sale, offer large sums for copies that may be purchased through private channels. Beauty of words and great writing are not dead, but it will need a literary world thoroughly Changed to Christ to rid us of the pernicious influence of a minority of authors who would sell their souls to the Devil.

The theatre and cinema are easy prey to those who would commercialize indecencies. Censors and police are vigilant in most countries to stamp our moral degeneracy in entertainments, but the appetite of a prurient minority demands indecencies, immodesties, and easy virtue in entertainments and is willing to pay well for them, so those who cater for this class of entertainment-goers use every device and subterfuge to give them what they want. Much that is not only against good taste but frankly harmfully obscene gets past the guardians of the morals of the entertainment public. 'Where there's a will there's a way' is proved constantly in the business, and films and plays are often produced publicly which make the public wonder whether any kind of censorship exists at all.

That pictorial art must shock to attract attention is the belief of some of those who have an artistic capacity. Modern art galleries and exhibitions exude suggestive nudity from their walls. Grossness is mistaken for artistry; blatancy for originality; indecency for truth, until the average person often wonders if these artists are half-wits who have never grown beyond the silly crudity of their childish sex-obsessions.

In this modern world it is believed to be impossible for any one who lives actively to lead anything approaching a virtuous life. How can one have untainted motives in the business world, for instance, when one has to compete with the lying misrepresentations of one's competitors who will stick at nothing to ruin one? How can one think modestly when literature, films, plays, and art rely on impurity to tickle the palate of a jaded public? How can one behave with purity when one is surrounded by people who find impurity of action the incentive to forgetfulness that we are not on earth for ever and 'live to-day for to-morrow we may be dead' a drug that deadens them to sensitiveness and remorse? What shame is there in incontinence when pseudo-scientific writers tell us to allow our instincts full scope if we wish, because that is being 'natural' and that being 'natural' is the best way to be happy?

The only Person who can answer these questions is Christ, and He cannot answer them for us unless we really want to know and will listen to what He tells us. How many people believe that though the world breeds impurity God can take it away? If we believe God can meet every temptation we must believe that God can keep us pure. He has never allowed a soul to suffer for resisting a temptation, although materially it may seem as if the results of that resistance have been a distinct loss to us. 'And lead us not into temptation' means 'take away from us the burden of temptation that appears too great for our human nature to resist'. How many of us realize that the Holy Spirit can enter and sanctify a mind, sweeping its darkest corners, opening spiritual windows that human means cannot move, letting in the cleansing sunlight, bathing the spiritual room that is within us all in the serenity of real purity? Feeding the mind on impurities is like feeding the body on tainted food. Because we know the consequences to the body of such foolishness we would not eat tainted food, why then do we feed the mind on impure food that must slowly but surely kill the soul? Kill it until, because the Holy Spirit has been destroyed within us, we say bitterly that there is no God?

3 . ABSOLUTE
UNSELFISHNESS

'Let each man do
according as he hath purposed in his heart;
not grudgingly or of necessity:
for God loveth a cheerful giver.'
2 CORINTHIANS IX. 7.

'And whosoever shall exalt himself
shall be humbled;
and whosoever shall humble
himself shall be exalted.'
MATTHEW XXIII. 12.

ABSOLUTE
UNSELFISHNESS

'But ye, brethren, be not weary in well doing.'
—2 THESSALONIANS III. 13.

*A*BSOLUTE unselfishness is only possible if we have absolute love; we can only be unselfish according to the love we bear towards the object of our unselfishness. This love is not necessarily admitted as love by the world. Sacrifice of ourselves or our interests to other people's interests, without thought of reward is, in itself, love, although we may not consciously recognize it as such when we are performing our act of unselfishness. There is more joy in absolute unselfishness than selfish people realize and it is not an unfruitful joy. Absolute unselfishness brings with it the knowledge that we are active for Christ, a zeal to go on and further Christ's rule on earth, and a certainty that, whatever we may give of ourselves, our time, money, talents, or our love, it is returned by God in the very best way for us. 'Cast thy bread upon the waters: for thou shalt find it after many days' is a positive fact. The bread of unselfishness that we cast upon the great ocean of human life which whirls around us *does* come back to us, not only a hundredfold in Christ consolation, but in the only sort of happiness that is of any use to us moderns in this world of illusions.

Why are we envious of other people? It does not need a genius to tell us. We want things other people have that we feel we could appreciate more than they do. We are dissatisfied; life is unfair to us. Are we not all made alike? That being so, why should other people be more fortunate? We want to be brilliantly coloured butterflies, not the drab moths that we think we are. As we become soured by failures and disappointments Life to us becomes one long wanting, wanting; then sooner or later our envy turns to hate of others and of ourselves. It is then some silly people say they wish they were dead, until they are awakened from their torpor of disillusion by a new and inspiring cause for another fit of fresh revitalizing hatred against something or somebody else. How they wallow in self-pity! No one understands them, they are misjudged mortals who 'have never had a real chance in life'. What, they ask, is life to them, anyway, but hell? And so they go on. Absolute Unselfishness? What rot! How can they be unselfish, they want to know, if they have to fight like wild beasts even to get what is due to them?—let alone have anything to be selfish about!

'Bear ye one another's burdens and so fulfill the law of Christ'. The curious thing is that the practice of Christ-Unselfishness takes away, as if by magic, all that self-pity, all those excuses we make to ourselves for our failures, all those feelings that we are being cheated, and, definitely, gives us in return the wonder of an inexplicable spiritual treasure, a description of which is impossible to put into words. It is curious because it is true, and some great truths are very curious to many of us ordinary people.

Some of us are spiritually proud with that pride that is inclined to make us thank God that we are not as other men are, and to despise those whom we feel are our inferiors in spirituality. It is that spiritual pride which gives us that sort of self-satisfaction that makes other people thank God they are not 'religious'. A virtuous feeling which comes with some self-sacrifice for the benefit of a faith we are members of, or the temptation to sin which we have, with much effort and self-restraint resisted successfully, often tends to give us that Pharisee attitude. Our spiritual selves are often selfish. When we have discovered a new way of spiritual living which makes us content, perhaps happier than

we have ever been before, we are often apt to ignore the fact
that there are many other people who, too, could, if we would
show then how, find a better way of living, not by our fault-
finding or superiority, but by real understanding of their difficulties and a simple demonstrative faith in Christ. We are so
inclined, too, to forget that our prayers are not for ourselves
alone and that they could be as beneficial to others as they can
be to ourselves. Even if our efforts spiritually to help others are
ineffective or if we realize that we cannot solve a social problem
which is beyond our human scope, we can ask for the prayers of
other people to unite them to our own. That is unselfishness.

In home-life unselfishness is a sure foundation for harmony.
It does away with friction and levels everything by love. Hatred
and mistrust of one relation for another can surpass in intensity
the hate and mistrusts unrelated people can have for one another.
Family feuds, caused by jealousy, pride, and suspicion have
wrecked many lives. Who amongst us does not know of a family,
if not our own, which is split by enmity? It is so very usual an
occurrence that in time hating our relatives often becomes a sort
of pastime and we are very pleased with ourselves when we have
scored some point in our favour in the game of hating those to
whom we are related. The silly spectacle of two people, closely
related, ignoring each other in public because they are playing the
hating game is too familiar to some of us to be funny any longer.
'Give and take' is a popular remedy for unselfishness that is supposed to be able to end these feuds, but the expression would be
of more practical use if the 'take' were not included. 'It is more
blessed to give than to receive.' It is miraculous what giving with
no thought of return can do to disarm the person who is opposed
to us. When we give to him without a self-motive there is no
hostile retort he can honestly make, whether our giving be essentially material, a point of argument, or a point of personal pride.
The practice of the Absolute Unselfishness of Christ is an unfailing remedy for family discord.

It is natural for growing children to resent parental control, which they think is bad discipline or selfish ownership, and to make up their minds to get away from home at the first opportunity. But what children brought up to value unselfishness and with the example of Christ before them would not understand and appreciate advice and wise control from parents who have not only instilled that unselfishness into them but practised it themselves?

Because it is founded on love, unlimited unselfishness between married people makes marriage proof against disagreements and divorce, and the bond between them grows stronger as the years pass. This mutual unselfishness can become, by practice, an instinct; one knows what the other needs without asking and supplies it without showing what the unselfishness costs the giver. Appreciation of the other's unselfishness does not lessen but grows as character develops. It is real comradeship, and love without comradeship is not marriage in the true sense of the word.

In these days pride is becoming a world-wide obsession. More than ever before people are judged and given place according to their possessions, rank, feats, and accomplishments. Even some kinds of humility are the worst form of pride. Many people are proud of being 'nobodies'. 'After all, I'm only a nobody' is a silly expression of pride we hear far too often.

'For what shall a man be profited if he shall gain the whole world, and forfeit his life? Or what shall a man give in exchange for his life?' Some national heroes are really world heroes; they bring, through their sheer pluck and determination, new possibilities of living to every one.

But who will deny that the modern mania for record-breaking is not often fostered by national selfishness, jealousy, and pride? If an airman of one country flies round the world or across a continent in a few days or hours a man of another country attempts to beat that record in a less number of days or hours; having accomplished that feat another airman of another country starts off to beat him. Dangers? Death? What are they when we are beating a record? Think of the prestige of our country, of the mayors and corporations who will turn out in their full regalia to greet us when we land; of the cheering crowds who would not be there to cheer if we had failed; think of our basking in the glaring limelight of publicity (at least until some one more intrepid or more unimaginative than us beats our record); think of the advertisement we bring to the manufacturers of the materials we use for our feat and the money they pay us for risking our lives to advertise their goods. What fun life is!

But where and when will this ridiculous world-wide mania end, whether it be for Olympic games that have no comradeship in their motives, stunt-flying, football cup-finals that are more notable for the size of the huge crowd watching than for the game itself, pole-squatting fools, non-stop dance records, starving men and women in barrels, or sporting matches in which the size of the purse is often of more importance to the public than the sportsmanship? In record making, or breaking, even a second can make one man greater than another; a quarter of an inch another man a national hero. We do not need to be carping spoil-sports, or to have great knowledge of crowd psychology, to envisage the great danger to civilization this change from healthy competition to widespread worship of the god of Selfish Pride and Jealousy this abnormal idolatry of feats has become. Other civilizations have worshipped that same god towards the ends of their glories. Is that a sign that we are towards the end of our civilization now?

Jealousy is selfishness. It is that extreme domination of self which is the most unprofitable side of mankind. It does nothing for the lasting advantage of any man and more to make the world as a whole less happy than any other failing. Jealousy is a collective sin, as well as an individual one. It can destroy a nation as easily as it can impel individuals to do things which they may regret for the rest of their lives. None of us knows to what end our jealousy about even a small and unimportant thing will lead us, a small jealousy can in time become an obsessing giant. Murder is no unusual result of a jealousy which has never been checked from its small beginnings.

To a certain degree we are all jealous and vain. Which of us can honestly say that we are not vain of our possessions, success, positions, self-restraint, liberty of action or thought, accomplishments, religious beliefs, agnosticism, goodness, or wickedness?—or jealous of other people's? The family that eat very little so that they can save enough to buy themselves a piano they cannot play because their neighbours have a piano they can play are not more foolish than we who give up things in our lives in order to be equal to our neighbours in any respect. Jealousy, envy, and pride, are the cause of our own little wars which we fight with our relations, friends, or neighbours, either in private or in public life. Before these petty wars with others can cease we must make peace within ourselves; we know it is as useless to compete with some one who refuses to compete with us as it is to play a game with some one who will not play. If we stop, the war stops; if we are not interested those who go on fighting find their joy and zest in the fight evaporating. Aloofness from wars of jealousy, envy, and pride does not necessitate our being self-satisfied; it merely requires spiritual common sense plus a sense of humour.

Selfishness contributes a great deal towards class hatred. Universal waste in these days of glaring poverty is criminal, but who is going to stop it? Governments, laws, revolutions? Those who have more than their fair share of worldly goods hate criticism. 'We don't waste,' they would say, 'even if we did, if it is ours why should not we waste it? We can do as we like with our own? Selfishness? Is it your business what it is? In your own way you are selfish too. So why should not we waste our money, food, clothing if we feel we want to?' Although there are many rich philanthropists who help the needy along, that is the attitude of some of those who spend as much on themselves in luxuries in a day as others can afford on bare necessities in a year. To these harmful few Absolute Unselfishness seems an impossibility or a remote fantasy of a disordered mind. They think they are owners by right of possession. How often some of us say that 'Possession is nine points of the law!' That is what selfishness is, when we allow our spiritual and material possessions to possess us. A person without wealth can be just as selfish as one with a fortune. We can and do waste our physical energies and spiritual possibilities as flagrantly as wealth is wasted; our spiritual potentialities for individual and universal good, as much as human life and materials, are wasted in abortive endeavours to make the world better by human means alone. Nothing can take away that vital invisible part of each one of us which is God's alone.

Because it is invisible some of us think that part of us is non-existent, forgetting that things we cannot see are often more important than things we can. By trying to the best of our abilities, under the direction of God, we can, if we will take to ourselves Absolute Christ-like Unselfishness, arrest this world-spread stupendous waste of good materials and equalize the positions of our fellow men. Neither laws nor civil bloodshed can ever accomplish this change to just administration of wealth and possessions. It is the duty of each one of us to bring Christ into the problem.

4 . ABSOLUTE LOVE

'*If I speak with the tongues of men*
and of angels, but have not Love,
I am become sounding brass, or a clanging cymbal.
'*And if I have the gift of prophecy,*
and know all mysteries and all knowledge;
and if I have all faith, so as to remove mountains,
but have not Love, I am nothing.
'*And if I bestow all my goods to feed the poor,*
and if I give my body to be burned,
but have not Love, it profiteth me nothing.'
1 CORINTHIANS XIII. 1–3.

'*By two wings a man is lifted up from things earthly,*
namely by Simplicity and Purity.
Simplicity ought to be in our intentions; Purity in our affections.
'*Simplicity doth tend towards God;*
Purity doth apprehend and as it were taste Him.'
THOMAS À KEMPIS.

ABSOLUTE LOVE

In loving thou doest well; in passion not,
Wherein true love consists not. Love refines
The thoughts, the heart enlarges; hath its seat
In reason, is judicious, and is the scale
By which to heavenly love thou mayest ascend.

JOHN MILTON.

BSOLUTE Love is the motive power for Absolute Honesty, Purity, and Unselfishness. We can have none of those qualities in their absolute without Absolute Love. If we have Absolute Love for God we have all those qualities for the world. We can be paragons of righteousness, but if we have not Love we are spiritually lifeless. Love begets love; and our active love to-day will go on spreading over life into the far future like the circles upon a lake when we throw in a stone. Love uplifts us more than any other quality; it is the colour in the pattern of earthly existence.

To every sensible thinking man and woman the life of Christ on earth should be irrefutable proof that His Absolute Love for mankind was, and is, an undying quality that even thousands of years cannot dim. That love which Christ showed us whilst He walked in flesh among men has gone on for nearly two thousand years, never getting out of date or ineffective. People are gradually realizing that mind is more important than, and can be as substantial in its effects as, matter. How much more important and real in its effects than either is love! Mind in many cases is dependent on bodily condition; an enfeebled body inducing an enfeebled mind. Absolute Christ Love is not dependent on any conditions; it needs no vast intellect or robust physical health to realize and use its illimitable powers; it is normal and practical, giving out and building up and is not an exclusive gift for the use of one type of individual more than another. It is the one indispensable part of existence that all the wealth there is, or ever has been, cannot buy. It helps those upon whom sorrow has suddenly cast a dark shadow, which seems can never be lifted, to get a right view-point for their future happiness; the continually troubled to realize that their eyes are focused on the side of life which inevitably leads to the no-man's land of utter despair, and turns their attention to the infinite possibilities of a future which has no one to say nay to them but God alone.

Absolute Love transcends everything; it envelops the world, but the world will not see it. Absolute Love is the language of God and Truth in Perfection. The realization that God loves us takes away all fears, doubts, regret and remorse, shame of the past, dread of the future. Such love passeth all understanding, bringing in its train infinite patience with man, enduring courage in life, and complete trust in Christ. If we could love God with a fraction of the love God has for us our eyes would be open to a new vision, not only for ourselves, but for all mankind.

'By this', said Christ, 'all men know that ye are my disciples, if ye have love one to another.' Disciples! Members of a fellowship of real equality! Absolute Love is not self-negation; it is using the best of ourselves for the best of other people and, in doing so, we realize that the best within us is a positive force for our own good as well as that of others. Many of us do not understand what fellowship means or that looking for self motives in people's good actions is killing the good within ourselves. Many people look for motives in kindnesses that are proffered them. 'What is he hoping to get out of it?' they often think when they have been shown an unexpected generosity, and then the good proffered to them loses its most potent asset, the good

Christ gave without thought of return or thanks.

Many people who give, put too much importance on thanks which are not so necessary to the givers of good as they suppose. 'I'll never do anything for him again,' a giver will say, 'why he never even thanked me!' Was Christ thanked for the greatest good He did—His becoming a man for us? When He was thanked by those upon whom He worked miracles He sent them on their ways feeling that He was happy that His belief and trust in His Father could, through Him, make them whole. Christ gave thanks to His Father, showing us that it is to God, the Fountain of all good, our thanks should be given. Should we not have others thank God for us than thank us alone? By that they are paying us the greatest tribute possible to be paid to man.

Absolute Love is wanted in the world to-day more than anything else. If civilization is not to decay utterly it is our vital need. This is not pessimism. Consciousness that Absolute Christ Love only can save us is the most optimistic piece of honesty we can face. The majority of people will not face squarely even the most pressing problems. They hope that in some way an unexpected salvation will appear from somewhere, sometime, somehow, soon, and put the world's affairs perfectly straight and, in consequence, with little or no effort on their part they will be quite happy and comfortable again. But it is not quite so easy as all that to bring civilization at its ebb-tide back to the full flood of content and prosperity. To make its scales balance again the world needs to face its problems honestly and to recognize what the power of Christ's love can do. How many people give more than a passing thought to the foolish administration of the world's, or even their country's affairs, the ineffectiveness of Godless governments and institutions and laws for which every individual is directly responsible as a citizen? Patriotism is not enough. Fearless, boundless love of God is the only key.

Love is not only an emotion. Love is understanding, and when we give understanding we give love. 'A loving heart', said Thomas Carlyle, 'is the beginning of all knowledge.' Who welcomes this knowledge of a loving heart? How many of us want to be troubled to realize that, in these days when poverty is a crime and charity is meted out with all the soullessness of the law, homeless honest men and women would rather remain homeless than accept help from soulless state machines they believe will cast an undying stigma on them? That workhouses, where charity has lost the blessed sweetness of its name, are in their very soullessness a punishment for poverty? That at night wrecks of humanity huddle together in the public places of great cities united in the common bond of homelessness, whilst only a few humanitarians, with real pain in their hearts for these flotsam and jetsam on the stream of human life, try to alleviate their lot in some measure, but without being able to reach the root of this canker in our civilization that should know no want? Do we really care that hunger-marchers, who march with class hatred in their very souls against those they believe to be their oppressors, find at their journey's end nothing that will give them back even their self-respect? Or that prisons, because of the lack of constructive moral regeneration, cause the prisoners to nourish fresh projects for the very crimes punishment is intended to stamp out? Do we care that prison life is often destructive, turning those who, because they believe the world has turned its back on them, into habitual criminals, when they might re-enter freedom wiser and better citizens? Do we think it is our business that reformatories and schools of correction leave on the young, who have taken the first wrongful step, a social blot they feel they can never clean themselves of? 'Go and sin no more' is of very little use to any one if his future has been destroyed and he is branded as an ex-convict to his dying day.

And yet, knowing all these things, are we like some people who still wonder why one class wars against another class and wish to get back to that time when the lower classes were inarticulate because they were uneducated, and the upper classes stolidly comfortable and content in their knowledge that pride of family, prosperity in business, outward respectability, and strict conformity to social demands were the backbone of the social system of that time? Being part of the system to-day we must realise that, in these times which change with the quickness and unexpectedness of a chameleon, that system has no deep roots. Education of the masses has loosened tongues, criticism, ideas, and dreams; working-class social revolutionaries are willing to die in order to put into practice reforms their forefathers could not have put into words not so very long ago. We must remember that no one can prophesy with certain knowledge or real foresight the nature of the change in the structure of social life that may come about even in our time but it is certain that events will go at a far quicker pace as the next few years pass, and that the end may bring a holocaust, the like of which has never been seen or imagined. If half these problems so near to all of us could awaken even a spurt of constructive action we should try to get down to the real solution by proving to the world that Christ, with His Absolute Love for mankind, can and will save, for the sake of a few, the many who will not even know Him.

It is those of us who call ourselves Christians who must demonstrate what Absolute Christ Love is before the world will accept it; who, whatever or whoever we may be, must accept Christ's Absolute Love as the fountain from whence the essence of our being springs. Our endeavours to make Christ Love the very air which our souls breathe will be our best endeavours to make this world a better and happier place for all to live in. It is of no use to ourselves or to any one to picture to ourselves Perfect Christ Love and what it could do universally and say it is pleasant to think of but impossible to use for the good of all, so why trouble about it at all? It will be our concerted efforts that will save us all from the unthinkable climax that unchecked class hatred may soon bring upon us, and unless real Christians determine now to give Christ Love full scope in their individual lives what chance of peace is there for the whole world in the future?

Christ is the natural arbitrator for world problems. If the world accept any other judge, the struggles to which many fine people are giving their lives to better the conditions of mankind will come to nothing; splendid ideals and great aspirations will become fainter in the memory than those dreams at night which are forgotten in the waking day; men and women who are now living lives of great example will have given in vain the best that is in them. The love of Christ is love which has intellect and judgment beyond any bounds which we can conceive; it is as applicable to-day as in those yesterdays that have long since become history. Christ Love is Absolute, recognizing the domination of no social system but only Truth and Justice; building up where destruction has prove fruitless, giving real understanding where discussions without Christ-influence only end in a deadlock. The Christ Love that can be within us, and can run our lives for us, can run the world. It is a force waiting to be directed upon all that goes to weave this web we call Civilization; it is the Absolute Love that can truly entitle us to call every man 'Brother'; it is under the influence of this Absolute Love only that we can all be the world's workers to carry out and complete, in God's good time, the Plan He has for this world, a Plan which far surpasses any conceived by man.

Absolute Love is the Absolute Love of God through Christ. It means not only the giving of our spiritual individuality, all the human best that is in us, but the receiving from God the peace of that quality of life He gave to the world when He gave us Jesus Christ, who understood and practised perfectly Absolute Love among Men. Love is not only doing but seeing. If we can see men as Christ saw them in His life on earth and sees them now, all things are possible unto us. To be actually and helpfully conscious of other people's existence, of the fact that they are like us, in that they are all separate individuals with urges, failings, strengths, opinions, desires, reasons, likes, and dislikes as we have, and to try to ally our own individuality to theirs, so that neither we nor they will be the weaker or the stronger, but partners in Christ, mutually understanding and forgiving, living together in perfect harmony of human and spiritual brotherhood, is to understand Absolute Love. Often, it is not so much what we give to others but what we give up for them that makes for harmony and that bond of real understanding from which love springs. God can and does give back to us so much more in return for that which we give up for our fellow men. No man has given up more for humanity than God could repay; within us all we have the inexhaustible wealth of God to draw on, a wealth which is a mine within us, the treasures of which become more precious the deeper we go below the material crust of the dark earth.

'Who is good except he be made so by loving?' asked St. Augustine. Radiating Absolute Love to all mankind makes for invulnerability to hurts and misfortunes, and unites us to the Holy Spirit. That is the art of living in perfection.

THE WORLD

'It is of the Lord's mercies that we are not consumed,
because his compassions fail not.'
LAMENTATIONS III. 22.

'The night is far spent, and the day is at hand:
let us therefore cast off the works of darkness,
and let us put on the armour of light.'
ROMANS XIII. 12.

'If it be possible, as much as in you lieth,
be at peace with all men.'
'But if thine enemy hunger, feed him;
if he thirst, give him to drink:
for in so doing thou shalt
heap coals of fire upon his head.'
ROMANS XII. 18 AND 20.

THE WORLD

*'The kings of the earth set themselves in array,
and the rulers were gathered together, against the Lord,
and against his Anointed.'*

ACTS IV. 26.

THE spirit of Anti-Christ has reared its head more bla-
tantly in the post-Great War years than ever before. The
Anti-Christ spirit is in every walk of life, and enemies
of Christ use every means in their power to crush Christianity.

The danger of the present Anti-Christs is that they are
playing upon the credulity of a tired and sick world which has
thoroughly degraded itself and now wishes to blame God for its
sins. The spirit of Anti-Christ is malignant. Like a fever which
obtains a firm hold of a physical body when it is in a low state of
health, the Anti-Christ spirit hopes to obtain a hold over this
weakening civilization. It will become far greater as the world loses
its spiritual vitality. It increases daily.

The entire world is pulsating with nervous fear, which is
deadly in its effects. It is very little wonder that the Anti-Christ
spirit is spreading over the world. The universe is in that condition when it feels that any kind of vital activity, wrong or right,
is better than dull monotonous inactivity. Millions are verging on
starvation or disillusioned by the rosy dreams of the future which,
held out to them by self-seeking so-called Christian politicians,
have never materialized, and they feel that if world reconstruction on old foundations is a hopeless dream violent destruction
of old forms is a better adventure than endless inactivity. To

them glorification of men is better than a God they believe has deserted them, even if He exists at all.

Does this incredible world chaos, out of which statesmen cannot show us the way, mean that this civilization must go the way of other civilizations which are now but legend? It is certain that this civilization cannot continue to live whilst its roots are rotting with fear, hate, and paganism. Must it pass into oblivion as have those other civilizations when they had reached the peak mark of degeneracy? Look at this Civilization. The physical and the material are glorified. Men and women risk their lives to accomplish feats that pander to national pride which has no spiritual significance. Nations are ruled by the hysteria of hero-worship; simplicity has given way to giantism in every aspect of life. 'Super' is the ambition for everything; in business, buildings, crowds, cities. Wars are gigantic massacres; peace is a gigantic hoax.

People are not only talking glibly about War but working for it. The universe is a huge munitions factory. Fear and spiritual negation keep that factory always at work piling up armaments ready for use at any moment. Humanity spends £200 every minute on armaments, and that in what is supposed to be a period of Peace! Armies are glorified by their nations; navies cost millions of money that could be used to better the living conditions of all. Pride is costly always but national pride in armaments is the most costly and senseless pride of the world at large. Whilst this pride remains Conferences and Leagues will remain a hollow mockery. No Great Power will disarm to any marked degree whilst its neighbour maintains its army and navy at War strength. That is called a defensive policy. Hostilities between nations, between your nation and the other nations, is going on at this minute; the trenches may not be visible, but the Spirit of War is there. In all respects the outlook of the world to-day is warlike, particularly in economics. The efforts of one state to squeeze economic subjection from another state is definite warfare. And among us is the Holy Spirit waiting to make

defences between man and man, nation and nation, fade into
oblivion so that we can all see ourselves as God sees us, His
Children.

We know that until God is the deciding factor in the nego-
tiations for Peace among Nations the League of Nations will
remain earth-bound. But just knowing that is not of any use; we
must see that our counsellors, our representatives, not only know
it, too, but that they act upon it and swiftly, unless chaos is to come
whilst we selfishly live our daily lives and wake up only when the
shouting and the tumult of the next war has commenced.

National isolation and self-complacency are stultifying spiritual and material progress. There is not, and there never has
been, a nation that could afford to be sufficient unto itself. The
Guidance of God as a working force can be more powerful than
any scheme divised by man for the amelioration of national or
world difficulties. God must be in our plan as we are in His.
Definitely there is no other solution to our difficulties.

Nations are afraid that Honesty is weakness when in its true
sense it is the essence of strength. Remember we cannot expect
our neighbour to be honest with us if he knows we are not being
honest with him. As with individuals so with nations and each
man has within himself the potentialities for world reconstruction and harmony.

Practical Christianity is the only possible solution to the
economic and peace problems of the world. *There is no other
solution. Every other method has failed and will always fail.*

Will any representative of a world power have the moral
pluck at the next Disarmament, Peace, or Economic Conference
to tell the assembly that no longer is he going to remain a passive
Christian but become an active life for Christ; that his work is
going to be founded on Christ's Honesty, Purity, Unselfishness,
and Love? Is there a statesman who believes in Christ suffi-
ciently to do this?

*And he shall judge between the nations, and shall reprove many
peoples: and they shall beat their swords into plow-shares, and their*

spears into pruning-hooks: nation shall not lift up sword against nation, neither shall they learn war any more, we read in Isaiah.

Think of the Spirit of Christ as the Direction of the League of Nations; of the Love that casteth out Fear which would emanate from the League; of Christ Peace for the World that would pass all understanding and enable mothers to feel that their children were free for ever from the monster of War. Think of homes that could be founded surely on the rock of faith and security in God; of the great minds that could devote their genius to bettering mankind instead of destroying it; of the humble ploughman as safe on his little plot of God's earth as the man in an impregnable castle. It may be an Oxford Group vision, but all great reforms for the welfare of mankind were visions once.

What mean ye that ye crush my people, and grind the face of the poor? saith the Lord, the Lord of Hosts.

Wars are not the invention of the man-in-the-street but of the man seated in a comfortable armchair behind bullet-proof walls. The aim of the Oxford Group is to penetrate those walls with a common-sense message from Jesus Christ; to Change the World to Christ by Changing lives; to make every one face squarely not only his own problems but World problems without fear or favour and to solve these problems by Changing those responsible for them. Ambitious? Yes, but what an ambition for you to have, too!

Y O U

'*I know thy works, that thou art neither cold nor hot:
I would thou wert cold or hot.*'
REVELATION III. 15.

'*Is reform needed? Is it through you?
The greater the reform needed,
the greater the Personality you need to accomplish it.*'
WALT WHITMAN.

'*Thou therefore, my child,
be strengthened in the grace that is in Christ Jesus.
And the things which thou hast heard from me
among many witnesses, the same commit thou to faithful men,
who shall be able to teach others also.
Suffer hardship with me,
as a good soldier of Christ Jesus.*'
2 TIMOTHY II. 1, 2, 3.

Y O U

'But if we walk in the light, as he is in the light,
we have fellowship one with another and the blood
of Jesus his Son cleanseth us from all sin.'
—1 EPISTLE JOHN I. 7.

THE Oxford Group offers Fellowship in Christ to the world; reborn souls to the Churches; a sane, practical Christianity to put right the spiritual and material problems which confront us. The Group knows no social distinctions and no spiritual laws but God's laws. It has a future for every individual, a determination to impress upon this civilization that God's plan is the only plan that is workable for the good of a world where each for all and all for each would not be a theoretical fantasy but a Christwise fact. The Group knows that every Life that is Changed to God is definitely one more important step towards putting the world right, and that every Changed Life is one more individual set free from man-made slavery to Christ-given freedom. It has workable Christ data for the governors, the influential, and the thinkers who work in their particular ways for the world; for those who are governed, in whatever human grade they may be, it has a practical message for their co-operation towards peace and on earth goodwill towards men.

Absolute honesty? Absolute purity? Absolute unselfishness? Absolute love? If we do not believe they are possible on earth we do not believe that Christ came on earth. He came as God to do for us what we cannot do for ourselves. He came as Man, as our Example, as the personification of God's Plan for each man and woman. We are Moderns. We have great men and women living among us. We have the benefit of great discoveries and inventions for our better living conditions. We have great scope for the Future. God is a world necessity, we must not remain in the clouds like many men who devote their lives to studying stars they cannot touch whilst the real secret of the Heavens lies unheeded at their feet. God is as modern to-day as He was through countless yesterdays and will be in infinite to-morrows.

Let us be Moderns with God; or soon we shall be nothing without Him.

Spiritual apathy now is not only an individual sin that will have a direct effect upon future generations, but a sin towards God.

Individual apathy is the best breeding-ground for national blunders. If the individual cannot see that Jesus Christ can lead nations out of Chaos into Universal Peace and Contentment, or will not act on it when he does see it, then the responsibilities of his nation's blunders can be laid at his door. 'He that is not with me is against me' said Christ.

On the individual in everyday life rests responsibility beyond his reckoning. On these shifting sands of life it is impossible to build a house called the Future entirely of hopes and dreams. In this swift-changing material world our possessions of to-day may be our debts of to-morrow. Events move *swiftly* now; stability of money and morals has gone beyond the recall of conferences and laws; Hysteria and Hate are the diseases of the world; Pace has taken the place of Sanity; our children are being born into a social madhouse.

The hour for a Christian Revolution approaches.

On the rulers of this world rest responsibilities, the outcome of which can either wreck civilization altogether or bring a new era of peace and prosperity for which our children will call them blessed. There are no two ways to a new world. The rulers can see by the present crisis that there are many ways to destruction.

They must see that there is only one way to reconstruction and that is the way of Christ.

This, every individual of everyday life, is *your* world. This is your life to use for God and humanity or to throw away—as you choose. You select your Rulers, your own governments; in that, you make your own laws; you are making your future wars; in you is the fate of nations, the peace and progress of the world.

Do you know of even one person whose life would be happier and more fruitful if it were guided by God? You do? One—two—a dozen? Then those lives are your responsibility. We cannot all be great thinkers, or talkers for God. But we can be Life Changers in the best way we can, with those abilities best suited for the purpose. In this Crisis the woman whose domain is her small household is just as important to God as the Ruler of a Nation; to all of us in our different ways God gives His Challenge for a new world. It is a Challenge to YOU.

To you is offered Fellowship in Christ; eager hands are held out to you; difficulties in the way are your own making; whatever may be keeping you from the fullness of material life need not keep you from the fullness of a Surrendered life to God. Which will you have, God or Chaos?

It is YOU who hold in your hands the future spiritual and material happiness of individuals, the awakening of all nations to a sane and reconstructive policy for the united Fellowship of all peoples. It is not a dream. It is a necessity that has no alternative if Chaos is not to come. You must lead your leaders.

You means all of us.

For YOU there is work ahead; real work that has no limitations or end that Man can foresee.

When your work here is finished there are for you those words of St. Paul:

'I have fought the good fight, I have finished the course, I have kept the faith.'

Notes

Notes

Notes

Notes

HAZELDEN INFORMATION AND EDUCATIONAL SERVICES is a division of the Hazelden Foundation, a not-for-profit organization. Since 1949, Hazelden has been a leader in promoting the dignity and treatment of people afflicted with the disease of chemical dependency.

The mission of the foundation is to improve the quality of life for individuals, families, and communities by providing a national continuum of information, education, and recovery services that are widely accessible; to advance the field through research and training; and to improve our quality and effectiveness through continuous improvement and innovation.

Stemming from that, the mission of this division is to provide quality information and support to people wherever they may be in their personal journey—from education and early intervention, through treatment and recovery, to personal and spiritual growth.

Although our treatment programs do not necessarily use everything Hazelden publishes, our bibliotherapeutic materials support our mission and the Twelve Step philosophy upon which it is based. We encourage your comments and feedback.

The headquarters of the Hazelden Foundation are in Center City, Minnesota. Additional treatment facilities are located in Chicago, Illinois; New York, New York; Plymouth, Minnesota; St. Paul, Minnesota; and West Palm Beach, Florida. At these sites, we provide a continuum of care for men and women of all ages. Our Plymouth facility is designed specifically for youth and families.

For more information on Hazelden, please call **1-800-257-7800**. Or you may access our World Wide Web site on the Internet at **http://www.hazelden.org**.